Canada at the WTO

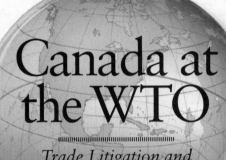

Canada at the WTO

*Trade Litigation and
the Future of Public Policy*

MARC D. FROESE

University of Toronto Press

LIBRARY AND ARCHIVES CANADA CATALOGUING IN PUBLICATION

Froese, Marc D., 1977–
    Canada at the WTO : trade litigation and the future of public policy / Marc D. Froese.

Includes bibliographical references and index.
Issued also in electronic format.
ISBN 978-1-4426-0138-3 (pbk.). — ISBN 978-1-4426-0152-9 (bound)

    1. World Trade Organization. 2. Arbitration and award, International — Cases.
3. Dispute resolution (Law) — Cases. 4. Canada — Commercial policy. I. Title.

HC1385.F75 2010   382'.92   C2010-900481-7

We welcome comments and suggestions regarding any aspect of our publications —please feel free to contact us at news@utphighereducation.com or visit our internet site at www.utphighereducation.com.

North America
5201 Dufferin Street
Toronto, Ontario, Canada, M3H 5T8

2250 Military Road
Tonawanda, New York, USA, 14150

ORDERS PHONE: 1-800-565-9523
ORDERS FAX: 1-800-221-9985
ORDERS EMAIL: utpbooks@utpress.utoronto.ca

UK, Ireland, and continental Europe
NBN International
Estover Road, Plymouth, PL6 7PY, UK
TEL: 44 (0) 1752 202301
FAX ORDER LINE: 44 (0) 1752 202333
enquiries@nbninternational.com

The University of Toronto Press acknowledges the financial support for its publishing activities of the Government of Canada through the Book Publishing Industry Development Program (BPIDP).

Designed by Daiva Villa, Chris Rowat Design.

Printed in Canada

This book is printed on recycled 100% post-consumer fibre paper.

For Gina and Arabel

Contents

Acknowledgements

First and foremost, I must acknowledge the immense contribution of my partner. Gina read drafts, discussed difficult topics, and helped me to clarify complex issues. I would never have completed this project without her unflagging encouragement and enthusiasm — even though our fields of study lie far apart. Sharing the long hours and intemperate obsessions of the *vita contemplativa* with her makes it all worthwhile. Of equal importance is my relationship with Daniel Drache. Our joint research projects have deeply informed my perspectives on trade and political economy. Daniel's mentorship has been more appreciated than he will ever know. That he has become a firm and lasting friend is positive proof of his generosity and my admiration.

Funding and administrative support were also critical to my research. The Social Science and Humanities Research Council of Canada provided funding for doctoral studies. The Robarts Centre for Canadian Studies at York University under the directorships of Daniel Drache and Seth Feldman provided office space and research funding for earlier iterations of this project. Special thanks are due to Robarts Centre Project Coordinator Laura Taman, who was an expert guide through the administrative maze that is so necessary to the operation of any large, research-intensive university. My colleagues at Canadian University College have been equally kind. I owe a debt of gratitude to the Faculty Research and Development Committee for continued funding of the project and to my colleagues Joy Fehr, Dean of the Division of Arts, and Loren Agrey, Academic Vice President. Over the past two years they have been understanding and generous to a fault.

Why Does the WTO Matter?

The World Trade Organization (WTO) is without a doubt the most important institutional development in the global economy since the end of the Cold War. Academic experts and policy analysts who follow current research in the study of globalization know that the creation of the WTO forever changed the international trade regime. But scholars and policy analysts have yet to develop a concrete understanding of how this new form of governance affects Canada. To be fair, Canadian policy experts know a great deal about the WTO. Many senior bureaucrats were present at its birth in 1995 and, indeed, played significant roles in its development during the Uruguay Round of trade negotiations. Since that time, Canada has become a sophisticated user of the WTO's dispute settlement panels. Nevertheless, there has been no systematic study of how the WTO's rules and decisions have in turn influenced Canada. It has been fifteen years since the WTO Agreement came into effect. It is time to take stock and ask a very important question.

How does dispute settlement at the World Trade Organization affect Canadian public policy? The conventional wisdom suggests that the WTO is a multilateral organization that manages and tames the unpredictable international marketplace by creating a common set of rules by which its members abide (Barton, Goldstein, Josling, & Steinberg, 2006). This process of governance contains a democratic trade-off in which Canada cedes a small amount of political sovereignty to the WTO, but this cost of trade liberalization is adequately offset by the beneficial impact on Canadian economic growth (Hart, 2002). The migration of some policy autonomy is to be expected in an era of global markets and increasing economic interdependence (Keohane, Moravcsik, & Slaughter, 2000). But policymakers ought to have a sound understanding of how the complex changes underway in the rapidly expanding, and increasingly global, market for goods, services, and information impact their own jurisdictions (Hall & Soskice, 2001).

Understanding the changes taking place at the global level requires a broad and multidisciplinary perspective that employs the research skills and interpretive knowledge of economists, political scientists, legal scholars, and a host of other disciplinary researchers. Studying the place of Canada in the new global trade environment requires becoming familiar with the language of economics and with a number of analytical tools, including the case study methods of political science and the historical and textual analyses of international law. By themselves, disciplinary approaches to studying the WTO tell us many useful things about global governance, but they do not provide a "big picture" of trade regulation.

Economists can model the behaviour of firms, states, and even negotiators sometimes, but they cannot tell us why some governments are much better at using WTO mechanisms than other governments. The easy answer is that rich governments can hire more experts than poor governments, but behavioural economists are starting to explore other questions, such as how having more (or less) information affects actor behaviour. This research could shed some light on why governments pursue agendas at the WTO that are rational in the short term but undermine national interests in the long term, as we see the United States, Japan, the EU, and Canada doing in agriculture negotiations (Akerlof & Shiller, 2009; Bagwell & Staiger, 2006).

Similarly, political scientists have a great deal to say about the asymmetries of economic and political power between members at the WTO (Drache, 2001). They trace the myriad ways that politics intervenes in economic processes (Dickins, 2006), but they seldom write about the primary method through which this intervention takes place—panel decisions. That is the realm of legal scholars. The meat and potatoes of WTO scholarship is undertaken by lawyers and law professors who participate as panellists and write about the intricacies of panel decisions (Abbott & Snidal, 1998). Yet they, in turn, have little to say about how these decisions are implemented and what the long-term implications are for states and markets (Howse, 2002).

This book occupies an unsteady middle ground. I do not claim it to be a disciplinary text. There will be much in these pages that pleases traditional scholars. There will also be some discussion that they consider to be incomplete, or perhaps oversimplified. This is the promise and peril of multidisciplinary scholarship—it can bridge the divides between many disparate pieces of scholarly knowledge, but it will never provide the completeness of disciplinary scholarship. However, if this book lacks in scholarly convention, it compensates the reader with a dynamic vision of the interrelationship between global politics, economics, and international law, set against the ever-changing backdrop of globalization.

The WTO has become a significant new international court, a primary site for multilateral interaction, and a controversial new governance concept in which international order is not necessarily accompanied by formal government. Despite or perhaps because of the high hopes of trading nations, the WTO has had a bumpy ride. As an international court for commercial disputes, the WTO has been remarkably successful. The rulings of dispute settlement panels are widely considered to be fair and balanced. Critics, however, rightly charge that few members actually use the dispute settlement mechanism because it is costly and requires a high degree of legal sophistication. Developing countries comprise three-quarters of the WTO's membership, and most have never taken a case "to court." As one of the primary sites of multilateral engagement, the WTO has attracted a large and growing roster of 153 member countries. Despite this apparent vote of confidence, most of these countries gain little from their multilateral investment besides the questionable prestige of membership. Indeed, it appears that many small nations join the WTO so as not to be left out. This represents a certain faith on the part of small nations that the big nations will act in the best interests of global growth. Or it may simply reflect a belief that large-scale multilateralism is the future shape of international economic decision making, much as the birth of the UN seemed to signal this shift in international security.

As a controversial new governance concept, the WTO seems to have at its heart a tension, which goes something like this: every single industrialized nation has used a large number of overtly protectionist measures to grow its industries, develop domestic markets, and help its firms compete abroad, yet the WTO's mandate and overarching institutional goal is free trade between nations. It is hypocritical in the extreme to deny these measures to developing countries, and it suggests a certain naivety about competition or, at the very least, a basic ignorance of history to argue otherwise. Nevertheless, with the fall of the Berlin Wall in November 1989, journalists and scholars from Thomas Friedman to Francis Fukuyama began to proclaim the triumph of capitalism, the failure of central planning, and the inevitability of a single global economy. In this utopian vision, trade liberalization leads directly to higher growth rates and more democracy. For disciples of the gospel of free trade, open borders are the best way for governments in the global south to provide the goods, services, investment opportunities, and political freedoms that their citizens require.

The WTO Secretariat has preached this gospel even though informed trade watchers know that the message is not based entirely upon the historical experiences of its leading members. Furthermore, the events that have transpired in the first decade of the twenty-first century have dispelled much initial optimism. Following the widely perceived failure of the economic policy template known as the "Washington Consensus," two wars in the Persian Gulf, and a global financial crisis, the world seems to have grown more complex, with fewer certainties. To add insult to injury, the WTO seems to be exhibiting many of the same organizational weaknesses seen in the UN. It is too large and cumbersome an organization to provide much in the way of leadership. Yet, if it were any smaller, it would not be truly representative of global society.

As a controversial new concept in trade governance, the WTO has been buffeted by the storms of circumstance as well as by political tempests whipped up by the practices of its members. Even so, there is something noble about the WTO's stated ambition for a truly level global economic playing field. It is true that, as tariffs were negotiated downwards and certain competitive practices declared to be unfair and therefore illegal, developing countries lost a number of potent weapons for competition and tools for growth. Yet, if they had not been taken off the table, developing countries would likely feel the sting of economic exclusion more now than ever before.

When the powerful Athenians stood before the colonists of Melos and offered them a choice — join us or die — they stated a basic truth about international relations that still echoes through the corridors of power today: "the strong do what they can and the weak suffer what they want" (Mingst & Snyder, 2008, p. 12). The WTO is a step removed from a model of international economic competition in which profit and power are the final arbiters of acceptable trade practice. Economists have known for quite some time that the mercantilist approach to development may have short-term benefits, but it can have a catastrophic effect on global markets, as it did following America's imposition of the Smoot-Hawley Tariff Act of 1930, which contributed greatly to the severity of the Great Depression.

Following World War II, the United States became a leader in the quest for a more stable economic order. Today, the United States, once thought to be the source of hegemonic stability and astute political judgment, has proven to be less a leader and more a laggard in key policy areas, including environmental protection, climate change, nuclear non-proliferation, international labour standards, poverty reduction, international health standards, and aid for pandemic-torn nations. Further, the leading template for economic growth that bore the imprint of cutting-edge American economic thinking has not had the intended effect. The Washington Consensus (so named because the United States Treasury Department, the World Bank, and the IMF, all based in Washington, DC, were in agreement on all the substantive issues) called for fiscal policy discipline, trade liberalization, privatization of state enterprise, and abolishing regulations that limit market competition.

These policy prescriptions were thought to contain the basic economic truth that economic growth is a function of free competition. The outcome was supposed to be societies in which marketization led to job opportunities, more consumer choices, and a higher standard of living for all. Of course, every consensus that generalizes across the very different experiences of dozens of disparate countries is bound to fail. Today, in every jurisdiction of the globe, the poor are poorer and the wealthy have more than they did forty years ago. It appears that not only did the Washington Consensus fail to lift the poor from misery, but it actually drove up economic inequality (Milanovic, 2005). In recent history, economic globalization (and the Washington Consensus to some degree) has not made the world a safer and friendlier place for a majority of its inhabitants; rather, it has made it more unequal, less stable, and less amenable to expert prognostication.

WHY THE WTO MATTERS
In theoretical terms, the WTO's rules have clarified a number of annoyingly fuzzy aspects of international trade regulation (Trebilcock & Howse, 2005). For example, trade disputes are now binding on both parties. No longer can countries ignore dispute settlement decisions that do not suit them — at least not without paying a penalty. For another, the relationship of developing countries to the international marketplace has been defined to a greater extent. The WTO's agreements categorize countries according to developed, developing, and least-developed status, and they have provided special and differential treatment for members according to their level of industrial development. Further, the plethora of non-tariff barriers to trade have been defined and catalogued, and, in some cases, limits have been negotiated. In this regard, the Dispute Settlement Body has been particularly helpful because its rulings provide precedent that informs future litigants.

In practical terms, trade litigation has created a new set of opportunities and constraints, which are often imposed on the Canadian political economy from outside (McBride, 2001). This is a fact that Canadians accept as part of the new reality of globalization. We understand that there is some correlation between increasing economic interdependence, on the one hand, and a certain loss of policy autonomy on the other. But must more governance always come at a cost to policy independence? Is it fatalism on Canadians' part to believe that the "good things" of trade governance, to quote Martha Stewart, always come at a high price (Byers, 2007)? I think that it is.

In the chapters that follow, the attentive reader will note that most constraints on Canadian policy autonomy come with corresponding opportunities. This situation poses a number of dilemmas for policymakers. Is policy constraint always adequately counterbalanced to policy opportunity? Even when Canada loses in dispute settlement, there is usually a silver lining. But what to do in situations when there is nothing to be gained and much to be lost? Or what about the larger dilemma? How should government approach the game of multilateral trade liberalization when Canada's immediate economic interests run counter to both our humanitarian values and our long-term development trajectory, as they do in agriculture negotiations?

Finally, is it not foolish to assume that rational markets and democratic governments can ever function in a mutually beneficial way? I am always mindful of the fact that people and their governments create markets, and not the other way round. It is this human element and corresponding humanitarian impetus that must be kept front and centre in any analysis of how Canada navigates the waters of economic globalization (Axworthy, 2003).

To map and track Canada's relationship to the WTO properly, our discussion will necessarily move between the national and international levels of analysis (Keohane & Milner, 1996). International agreements, legal conventions for state-to-state relations, dispute litigation, the efforts of domestic interest groups, and the strategies of national policymakers converge within the WTO's orbit. Members pursue disputes against trading partners according to the legal rules contained in the WTO Agreement. They also look to the supranational level to legitimize or disallow certain policy agendas. It is difficult to get a fix on the precise position of the WTO vis-à-vis its member states because its unique mix of trade law, multilateral negotiation, and binding dispute settlement has no precedent — not in the aborted International Trade Organization, first envisioned in the 1940s, nor in the GATT framework that regulated trade for almost fifty years after World War II (Hudec, 1999b).

I have developed an approach to analysing trade litigation based upon Susan Strange's concept of a "network of bargains" that frames international political economic interaction (Strange, 2003).

The many different actors at play in trade disputes form a network of interests that can be mapped using a case study method. The WTO is a big step forward for global trade. Its rules may benefit some nations more than others, its dispute settlement decisions may seem somewhat arbitrary at times, and its tangible benefits for developing countries may appear to be negligible, but none of these issues should obscure the most important fact about trade governance. In a global economy in which the strong do what they can and the weak suffer what they want, some governance is better than no governance at all. And with the right amount of political will, the WTO's inadequacies can be remedied. The first step is for members to take stock of their membership—what's going right, what's going wrong, and where is there room for improvement?

This book is divided into eight chapters. The first introduces a number of key issues that arise from the study of the WTO. There are a number of widely believed myths about WTO participation that should be done away with straightaway, and, of course, there are a number of important facts that all scholars of international trade must keep in mind when studying the impact of the WTO on one of its member countries.

The following five chapters provide case studies of Canada's experience in the dispute settlement system. The cases are organized around the major legal principles that were dealt with by the dispute settlement panels. Chapter 2 deals with the softwood lumber trade war with the United States and examines the WTO rules regarding anti-dumping trade remedy action governed by the Anti-Dumping Agreement and governmental support for industry found in the Agreement on Subsidies and Countervailing Measures. Chapter 3 examines the contentious issue of government monopolies in global trade. The Canadian Wheat Board has been one of the most successful wheat marketing boards in the world, and it has developed a strong brand for the products produced by western Canadian farmers. It is also considered to be a fundamentally anti-competitive institution by American wheat producers.

Chapter 4 continues the discussion of subsidies through a different lens—namely the lens of trade in high-tech products and Canadian competition with Brazil for the lucrative market for regional jets, narrow-body aircraft designed for short flights between regional hubs. Chapter 5 returns to the important theme of Canada–US relations by examining the notorious "magazine case," in which the United States successfully argued that Canadian law discriminated against American magazines and violated the General Agreement on Tariffs and Trade (GATT) Article III (the principle of national treatment), which establishes that imported goods should be taxed and regulated no differently than domestic goods once they have entered the local market.

The last case study analyses the way that dispute settlement may impact future policy decisions around intellectual property. The best example of the way that dispute settlement may have a chilling effect on humanitarian intervention is Canada's legislation that allows generic drug manufacturers to produce brand-named HIV medications for countries in Africa. The law is an ineffective piece of legislation, partly, because important patent disputes that Canada has lost at the WTO have contributed to an environment in which Canadian policymakers are more concerned with staying on the right side of patent enforcement than they are with getting much-needed medicine to desperately poor Africans. It appears that dispute settlement impacts not only existing legislation. It also has important implications for the future of public policy as well. Organizing these prominent disputes around key points of international trade law allows us to examine the way that international treaty becomes public policy, and the way that the international level plays an increasingly important role in the shaping of Canada's law and policy.

The final chapter draws several lessons from the case studies and speculates about the future of Canada's relationship to the World Trade Organization. Is it possible to create an international system in which international relations are fair and equitable for all parties? Is it desirable to develop a system of law that operates beyond the reach of citizen representatives? Are we already beyond the point at which these questions are still relevant? I do not think that we are. How a country participates in multilateral organizations should be decided not only by the best empirical evidence but also by the values and principles that country claims to represent in the international society of states. Policymakers have begun to develop a number of calculated and creative approaches to defining our place in the expanding universe of public international law. Therefore, addressing the unanswered questions that surround Canada's relationship to the international trading system is a timely project with large implications for the future of public policy.

CHAPTER ONE

Myths and Facts about the World Trade Organization

implicator

Canada is deeply interested in the well-being of the World Trade Organization (WTO), and our policymakers are convinced that trade multilateralism is a key component of Canadian competitiveness. Canada's economy depends upon a predictable system of international law for trade and investment. Even so, our involvement at the WTO has been intensely debated by academics and policymakers because the institutionalization of international trade governance forces governments to steer a tight course between the goals of multilateral participation and the domestic responsibilities of the modern welfare state (Krikorian, 2005).

There are a number of myths that have sprung up around the WTO. There are also a number of corresponding facts that need to be kept in mind throughout this study because so much controversy surrounds the global trading order. Thoughtful students of global politics cannot help but criticize the current global order. Trade liberalization has contributed to a rise in global inequality and has done little to lift the destitute out of misery. On the other hand, the growth of a truly international set of rules for the conduct of trade is a major step forward for the international society of states. Whether this regime will prove to be an enduring form of progress has yet to be seen.

MYTH: *The WTO is a form of global constitution for trade.* Where to place WTO law in the pantheon of international law is the main challenge facing legal scholars. One perspective that has been articulated recently emphasizes the constitutional nature of WTO trade agreements. There are two iterations of this perspective. On the left of the political spectrum, the constitutionalism argument has been made best by critical political economists such as Stephen Gill (1995), who have emphasized the WTO's role in creating standards that discipline the policies of member governments. This perspective is mainly concerned with the social impacts of trade and the way that the interests of rich economies are translated into trade treaties that may not be in the interests of poor countries, workers, and the environment.

A more mainstream approach to studying the constitutional elements of international economic law aims to uncover and understand the values that underpin interaction among states in the global economy. International lawyers John McGinnis and Mark Movsesian (2000) argue that the WTO should be understood as a supranational constitution that can simultaneously promote international trade and domestic democracy. They argue that the task facing the WTO is the task facing all constitutions: to encourage open markets and democracy — while resisting the attempts of politicians, bureaucrats, and special interest groups to hijack governance institutions for their own purposes. Free trade creates wealth for nations they argue, a fact reflected not only by rising levels of global trade but also by the large number of democratically elected national governments that favour free trade policies. Nevertheless, because some industries suffer because of free trade, those business owners and workers agitate for protectionist measures. Such interest groups often command a disproportionate power in national politics, and, as a nation becomes wealthier through trade, the incentives to agitate for industrial protection increase.[1]

The WTO's battle against protectionism is waged through a legal system that has a mandate to resolve claims concerning discriminatory measures but has limited authority over sovereign states.[2] In this way, the current legal model is comparable to the eighteenth-century American federalist model of government, which was intended to be a practical set of rules for trade between colonies that promoted prosperity and reflected majority will. A central concern of the American founding fathers is reflected in James Madison's warning against allowing industrial interests to decide major issues of public policy. "Shall domestic manufactures be encouraged, and in what degree, by restrictions on foreign manufactures? are questions which would be differently decided by the landed and the manufacturing classes, and probably by neither with a sole regard to justice and the public good."[3]

McGinnis and Movsesian argue that the WTO enhances democracy at the same time that it smoothes market distortions, a perspective that most scholars would consider to be optimistic, to say the least. It is more accurate to say that free trade is an *ideal* but has never been fully realized (Ruggie, 1994). Many factors stand in the way of global free trade, and absolutely free trade in everything that businesses produce would probably not be desirable. Flows of foreign goods and services would destabilize governments and make the secure provision of food difficult. Military defence capabilities, which rely increasingly upon technology developed with government support, would be seriously undermined. Labour markets in some parts of the world would collapse, and government provision of public goods, such as health care in the Canadian context, would become practically impossible. Certainly, the institutional goals of the General Agreement on Tariffs and Trade (GATT) and of the WTO have always been to better manage the current trading system and liberalize the markets of member countries gradually.

Scholars are right to note that the international level of governance has become increasingly important since the end of World War II. The past fifty years have seen a massive growth in the size and substance of public international law. Treaties, judicial tribunals, and standard-setting organizations are proliferating at a rapid rate. Some of the most impressive milestones of the past decade are the international ban on landmines (1997), the International Criminal Court (1998), and the Earth Summit in Rio de Janeiro (2002), which spawned six international environmental agreements on the issues of biodiversity, climate change (the Kyoto Protocol), desertification, and the sustainability of migratory fish stocks, among others (Cooper, 2004). Even so, there has never been a comfortable fit among the dozens of treaties, conventions, diplomatic understandings, and legal principles that comprise the body of public international law. In fact, a recent report released by the United Nations International Law Commission describes the current system as the "fragmentation of international law" and finds that, even if states would like a more coherent system of public international law, it does not yet exist (UNILC, 2006, p. 245). The WTO is a very important feature of the global economy, but it does not now, nor will it ever, possess constitutional powers.

MYTH: *The WTO punishes countries that do not adhere fully to international trade agreements.* Following the birth of the WTO in the mid-1990s, civil society groups became increasingly enraged by what they considered to be heavy-handed bully tactics on the part of the WTO (Bello & Kwa, 2003). They cited as evidence the closed-door "green room" sessions of trade negotiations in which wealthy countries pushed hard for trade concessions from developing nations. Trade sceptics also argue that the WTO punishes countries that do not comply with dispute settlement panel decisions and that WTO rules "lock in" these decisions because panel reports do not have to be ratified by the membership.

The first charge is answered in more detail in the following pages. The second charge, that the WTO can punish member countries, is a distortion that likely stems from early attempts to understand the new rules for compliance. In actuality, failure to comply with a panel decision means that the disputant may file a charge of non-compliance with the Dispute Settlement

Body. If non-compliance is proved, the WTO may authorize the withdrawal of certain trade concessions. For example, when Canada sued Brazil over its export credit policies for the sale of Embraer jet aircraft, Brazil was particularly reluctant to comply with the ruling. Canada sought and received a judgment of non-compliance and was authorized to remove trade concessions on a number of Brazilian products that were exported to Canada. It should be noted that, in this case, Canada did not remove those trade concessions but rather held the possibility as a negotiating card to be played in future talks with Brazil. Of course, Canada had also lost a case at the WTO in which Brazil attacked Canadian policies for financing aircraft deals brokered by Bombardier. Canada also failed to comply with the dispute settlement panel decision, and Brazil was likewise authorized to withdraw concessions to Canadian goods. In essence, these compliance judgments cancelled each other out. Clearly, cases are frequently complicated, and it is not always clear which member is guilty of foot-dragging, non-compliance, or even dirty trade tricks and which is the innocent and aggrieved party.

The withdrawal of trade concessions is a serious undertaking with potentially significant economic ramifications, and it is only a measure of last resort to gain compliance. Between countries with dense trade ties, the withdrawal of trade concessions in other sectors can be a powerful incentive to comply with the panel report, but between partners with sparse trade ties (such as Canada and Brazil), it is less useful. Governments may decide to bear the costs of foregone trade concessions (especially if those costs are not very great) in order to avoid the greater costs associated with compliance.

As for the charge that the WTO locks in its legal decisions thereby forcing members to comply with decisions that have been made in a forum beyond the reach of democratic publics, the critics have a point. The WTO rules do not require that a panel report be ratified by national public entities or member governments before it is adopted by the Dispute Settlement Body. In fact, the opposite is true. The WTO's reverse consensus mechanism requires membership approval for the removal of a panel decision, but, outside such an extraordinary situation, approval of panel reports is automatic. Nevertheless, the more strident voices arguably misunderstood the nature of the WTO system. The WTO, like the UN, does not have a police force. It cannot force members to adopt dispute settlement panel decisions. In fact, many defendants never fully comply with rulings. And even when they do comply, it is often through a compromise brokered through bilateral talks with the disputant, as happened in the litigation between Canada and Brazil.

The challenge facing the WTO is the challenge facing all courts—its role is limited to the sphere of law, yet it works in a political environment (Ehlermann & Lockhart, 2004). Its dispute settlement mechanism operates at arm's length from trade negotiations, much like a national court's relationship to the legislative branch of government. But that is where the similarities to national government end. In fact, because the WTO is designed for use by sovereign states, comparisons to national court systems are superficial and wildly inaccurate. In order to demonstrate this basic fact, here is what the WTO system looks like when compared directly to that of a national government.

If the WTO system were translated directly into a national jurisdiction, it would look like a court separated from agenda-setting or policy-making capacity—a libertarian's dream perhaps but, in reality, a cumbersome and impractical arrangement. Its legislative arm would be small and prone to protracted conflict. In place of an executive, it would make do with a skeleton crew of bureaucrats. The court would operate with greater effectiveness than the legislative arm of government, but it would not be able to rely upon the executive branch to enforce panel decisions effectively. In fact, the final compliance tool available to members, Article 22 of the Dispute Settlement Understanding (DSU), which authorizes the suspension of trade concessions, is recourse to self-help. Our hypothetical court would essentially tell parties, who were unable to collect their judgment, "Sorry, we've done all we can do." Usually, states are governed by legislators who are guided by judges in their creation and application of law, but this state would be governed by judges guided by fractious and self-interested legislators. Clearly, the WTO system cannot be compared to national systems of government. In fact, comparisons of this nature frequently lead students astray because they do not comprehend the goals of international law, nor the realities of a system predicated upon the voluntary compliance of sovereign states (Charnovitz, 2002).

How then should we think about relations between states in the international trading system? Is the WTO simply more of the old GATT—the General Agreement to Talk and Talk? If states are sovereign, what gives international law its force and effect? The legitimacy of the international trading system is rooted in "the agency of states ... and the capacity for collective action that states facilitate" (Schneiderman, 2000, p. 783). Let us take a look at the Internet to illustrate this point. Most people are at least familiar with e-Bay, and many have purchased goods or services through this huge, online auction house. Imagine yours is the winning bid, and you are suddenly struck by buyer's remorse. You have paid too much for something you don't really want. What stops you from simply walking away from the computer? Worse still, what if you got a great deal, and the seller is unwilling to sell the item for such a low price? Despite a lack of coercion, most people honour their contracts, even if they don't feel very good about it. E-Bay maintains a number of tools to ensure your compliance, including a system for tabulating the reputations of buyers and sellers. When someone buys or sells, other e-Bay users can rate their interaction with that person. Were they prompt in their payment? Were the goods received in the mail the same ones bid on? Heavy users of e-Bay pride themselves on their high reputation rankings, and they understand that failure to meet their contractual obligations in this instance will hurt their ability to use the auction house effectively in the future. The same is true of states that comply with international agreements. Legal scholars have found that most states comply most of the time with agreements that they have signed (Chayes & Chayes, 1995). The reasons for compliance are not always clear, but the "e-Bay effect" is certainly part of the explanation. Reputation matters in the multilateral trading system.

MYTH: *All countries benefit equally from participation at the WTO.* Although trade rounds are frequently considered in terms of what countries lose, negotiations are structured in such a way that, at least in theory, consensus on the final outcome derives from what all countries gain. The reality is not so simple. The WTO is a knowledge-based institution, and countries that are able to manage information and use it effectively are more successful in negotiation and dispute settlement (Ostry, 2006). It stands to reason that rich countries that can field more legal talent tend to dominate at the WTO. In this way, we can speak of the unfairness built into the WTO system, an unfairness that stems from basic inequality in the distribution of resources and wealth.

Political influence and market power are also significant factors in the process of liberalization, and they need to be examined as such. However, it serves nobody, least of all developing countries, when scholars and activists are sloppy in the way they analyse the WTO. We would be naïve to assume that diplomatic bullying never takes place at the WTO. However, much like spying on closed-door proceedings at the UN, backroom arm-twisting at the WTO is a by-product of high-stakes international negotiation and is perhaps inseparable from other, more visible forms of "diplomacy."

What about the domination of small economies by big ones? Wealthy countries, such as the United States, account for the largest portion of global trade and have championed a number of recent agreements that, by their very nature, benefit highly developed economies more than they benefit less developed ones. A good example is the Agreement on Trade-Related Aspects of Intellectual Property Rights (TRIPs). TRIPs sets patent term lengths and attempts to harmonize international rules pertaining to the enforcement of intellectual property rights. Intellectual property was a key American concern in the Uruguay Round of trade negotiations, and it is unsurprising that it became part of the global trading system with the conclusion of the round in 1994. Because the United States is among the world's foremost innovators, American multinational corporations, from IBM (business electronics) to Pfizer (pharmaceuticals) to Boeing (jets and aeronautics systems), derive an increasing portion of their profits from patented inventions.

If the world economy develops the way that many economists think it will, the TRIPs Agreement will benefit poor countries as they develop information economies. Unfortunately, another caveat is necessary. The reality is that today's wealthy innovators are yesterday's shameless appropriators. Some of the biggest firms in the global north got their start as borrowers of the ideas, processes, and knowledge of others. The best example of this is Walt Disney. Few people know that *Steamboat Willie*, the film that introduced Mickey Mouse, is based upon Buster Keaton's film, also released in 1928, entitled *Steamboat Bill, Jr.* Disney was one of the great geniuses of the twentieth century, and a part of his brilliance was his ability to bring together many different types of information widely available in the entertainment environment around him and make something new (Lessig, 2004). At that time, intellectual property rights were not as strict as they are now, and many innovators copied each other in an attempt to develop the perfect combination of product and presentation to please audiences.

When critics of the WTO argue that tighter intellectual property rules are an attempt by rich countries to kick the ladder out from under developing economies, they may have a point. Of course, the problems of equal benefit are not limited to procedural issues and intellectual property rights. Normative concerns relating to disparities in wealth and income and negotiating trouble spots in agriculture and services are also worrisome. A global economy of vast wealth inequalities is particularly prone to social and economic injustice, and these injustices play themselves out on a micro-diplomatic scale in the many different bargaining fora at the WTO — from liberalization negotiations to discussions on procedure and practice.

Despite its many well-documented inadequacies, the myths that surround the WTO are the sort that plague all new forms of international governance. Will it overstep its bounds? Will it produce fair and equitable outcomes for all members all the time, or will it only work the way it should for some members some of the time? Is it a better alternative to what was in place before? We have established that the WTO cannot be seriously considered to be a global constitution for trade. Nor is it an autonomous actor that disciplines its members whenever they step out of line. Most controversially, the arm-twisting and bullying that take place at the WTO are not the fault of the organization itself, although treaties that clearly benefit wealthy countries more than poor countries are part of the global trade architecture. Blame ought to be handed out to the members that use these tactics to assure that small countries fall into line. In order to get to the bottom of the misunderstandings about the WTO, we now need to look at a few key facts about the international trade regime.

FACT: *The WTO is an intergovernmental organization.* This means that only states have legal standing at the WTO. As such, it is a platform upon which sovereign states (represented by their governments) may resolve disputes and pursue collective goals. The authority of intergovernmental organizations (IGOs) comes from their members. The WTO is designed as an umbrella organization to administer a growing roster of international trade treaties, the most important being the General Agreement on Tariffs and Trade, which is the oldest trade treaty that governs the international trading system. In 1944, a year before the end of World War II, delegates from 44 Allied nations met at the Mount Washington Hotel in Bretton Woods, New Hampshire to begin to negotiate the creation of an international economic order to replace the dysfunctional interwar system. The International Bank for Reconstruction and Development, also known as the World Bank, and the International Monetary Fund were both planned at this historic conference. A third institution, to be called the International Trade Organization, was also planned, and it would have been a more comprehensive organization than the WTO is today, with provisions for labour and investment standards in addition to those for trade regulation.

Following the war, the United States Congress failed to ratify the International Trade Organization's charter. Without the signature of the world's largest economy, the International Trade Organization faded away, leaving the General Agreement on Tariffs and Trade (GATT) in an ambiguous position. The agreement had been signed by 23 nations, including Canada, but it had no formal institutional apparatus for administration. The GATT continued to exist without the formal institutional structure of its defunct parent organization for almost 50 years, until the creation of the World Trade Organization at the end of the Uruguay Round of trade negotiations in 1994.

The World Trade Organization is an umbrella institution that administers 60 different agreements. In legal terms, the WTO is made up of a single overarching agreement: the Agreement Establishing the WTO. This agreement is itself constitutive of three separate agreements that cover broad areas of trade. The GATT was joined by the General Agreement on Trade in Services (GATS) and the Agreement on Trade-Related Aspects of Intellectual Property Rights (TRIPs) in 1995. The GATT and the GATS have been clarified and developed through a number of extra agreements and annexes that regulate a wide variety of trade issues, from investment to health regulations for farm products and even telecommunications services. Following

Figure 1.1. *WTO Law*

The umbrella agreement	The Agreement Establishing the WTO		
The broad principles	**GATT**	**GATS**	**TRIPs**
Additional agreements and annexes	Agriculture, Sanitary and Phytosanitary measures (health regulations) Textiles Technical barriers to trade Investment measures Anti-dumping measures Customs valuation methods Pre-shipment inspection Rules of origin Import licensing Subsidies and countermeasures Safeguards	Movement of people (for the purpose of providing services) Air Transport Finance Shipping Telecommuni-cations	No additional agreements or annexes

these extra agreements are the schedules of commitments that delineate the specific commitments made by members. Under GATT, these schedules take the form of binding commitments on tariffs. Under GATS, members make commitments to allow access to the markets by foreign service providers.

Additionally, the WTO administers two plurilateral agreements on civil aircraft and government procurement. These are agreements that have been signed by a number of members but are not part of the single undertaking of WTO membership. (See Figure 1.1.)

The WTO is a stand-alone institution, which means that it is not part of the United Nations family of intergovernmental organizations. In this way, it has more in common with the World Bank and the International Monetary Fund than it does with the World Intellectual Property Organization (WIPO) and the UN Conference on Trade and Development (UNCTAD), which are part of the United Nations' family of institutions. The WTO is responsible for the organization and facilitation of trade negotiations, the settlement of trade disputes, and the periodic review of members' trade policies. The director general is the public face of the organization. He or she (although they have all been male so far) is the foremost bureaucrat in the WTO Secretariat and acts as a master of ceremonies, dealmaker, and confidant to members. All told, the WTO employs about 500 individuals; most are employed in some sort of research capacity. The WTO has a surprisingly small payroll for such a significant international organization.

FACT: *Members may decide when to launch a round of trade negotiations or when to take a case to the Dispute Settlement Body for arbitration, but WTO governance still imposes significant checks on state autonomy.* Most of the world's nations are already members—Cape Verde became the 153rd member in 2008. A few states, most notably Russia, are not. Members understand that participation in the world economy is enhanced by the development of rules for trade, standards of conduct, and a juridical regime for adjudicating disputes. Nevertheless, membership in the WTO does not come cheap. Hoekman and Mavroidis (2007) describe five areas where WTO rules limit the regulatory autonomy of member states. First, the WTO regulates the trade in goods. The WTO's historic mandate is the lowering and eventual elimination of tariff barriers to trade. Along with this mandate, it administers a host of multilateral agreements pertaining to trade in goods, including agreements on the use of technical standards and the application of retaliatory measures if a member is the victim of unfair trading practices.

Second, the WTO regulates the worldwide trade in services. Flows of commercial services were worth a whopping 6.3 trillion dollars in 2007, up from about 3 trillion dollars in 2000, according to the WTO's statistical databases. The General Agreement on Trade in Services (GATS) came into force in 1995, and it governs many aspects of the international flow of tradeable services, such as construction, business consulting, and international banking. The regulation of trade in services has potentially far-reaching effects, and states have been reluctant to enter into in-depth negotiations under the GATS because there are so many possible unintended consequences attached to this largely unexplored governance terrain.

Autonomy is not an all or nothing proposition, and states maintain shifting levels of policy capacity across numerous issue areas. Most members have developed unique and complex patterns of public and private service provisions within their national jurisdictions. For example, consider the differences in the way that health, education, and financial services are organized in Canada and in the United States. In Canada, there is a much larger role for government in health care. Most universities are public institutions, and the financial services sector is dominated by strictly regulated chartered banks. The United States has its own pattern of public regulation, with different rules for the organization of banking. The health sector has much more room for private business than it does in Canada. The United States also has a thriving postsecondary education sector that is dominated by a private liberal arts college model of service provision. In Canada, there are only a handful of private postsecondary education providers, and none is as prominent as Harvard, Princeton, or Yale in the United States. Add to this the issues surrounding service provision across the Internet, not to mention emerging issues in the energy and environmental sectors, and we begin to realize the size and scope of the task at hand. These complexities are compounded across the dozens of members at the WTO, and they suggest that many years will pass before services are liberalized to the extent that goods are, if in fact that level of market openness ever occurs.

Third, the WTO limits member autonomy by setting a standard for the protection and enforcement of intellectual property rights. The regulation of intellectual property is a new area of governance for the international trading system. The basic goal of TRIPs is to ensure that inventors receive a uniform level of protection across member jurisdictions. Before the Agreement on Trade-Related Aspects of Intellectual Property Rights came into force in 1995, intellectual property rights were minimally regulated at the international level, and there were no integrated international enforcement measures to ensure standards (White, 2005). The World Intellectual Property Organization (WIPO) provided a forum for the harmonization of IP rights between signatory countries but policing enforcement was largely voluntary.

The Office of the United States Trade Representative began the trend of linking IP rights to international trade when officials, having grown frustrated with piracy and lack of security for American industrial patents, began to enforce American patents unilaterally in the United States Court of International Trade under "Special 301" provisions (Mercurio, 2004). The TRIPs Agreement, while deeply unpopular in the global south (southern hemisphere), promised an end to unilateral American action on the patent front, and WTO dispute settlement was considered a better prospect than defending government action, or lack thereof, in an American court. TRIPs harmonizes IP treatment amongst all member states; patents must be protected for a term of 20 years. Before, every member of the WIPO set independent patent term limits.[4]

Fourth, the WTO acts as a court for the settlement of disputes. Members voluntarily take their disputes to the WTO for resolution, but they agree to abide by the findings of the panel, regardless of whether it decides in their favour. Dispute settlement has been one of the most controversial and successful aspects of the WTO (Allee & Huth, 2006). It is controversial because it is creating a body of case law that is not under the purview of any national government. To citizens in the Anglo-American and Commonwealth democracies especially, this smells of judicial activism and the tyranny of bureaucracy. Yet the system has been remarkably successful; members accept that WTO rulings are binding, and they are generally regarded to be of high-quality legal reasoning.

Why is it that governments and citizens are seemingly divided on the efficacy of WTO dispute settlement? It is most likely because governmental bureaucrats measure dispute settlement success differently than does civil society. For governments caught up in costly and complex disputes, opinions of expert panellists guided by international agreements are not only helpful but often instrumental to resolving disputes. Although the WTO's Dispute Settlement Body does not solve all disputes that are filed, its complaint resolution rate is high enough for governments to invest resources in it (Bown, 2004). Citizens' groups, on the other hand, are concerned by the lack of democratic representation at the international level. Although the most powerful governments at the WTO are democratically elected, national publics rarely, if ever, vote on whether their countries will be bound by trade agreements. The democratic process remains at a distance from the trade negotiation process. For governments, this is a good thing because it allows cool-headed experts to craft treaties and settle disputes. For civil society, the growth of governance without representative democracy at the international level is a troubling development.

To a certain extent, the creation of a dispute settlement mechanism was the logical outcome of the development of the GATT, which began as a 23-member body at the first round of negotiations in Geneva in 1947 and grew into a 125-member body by the beginning of the Uruguay Round 39 years later.[5] However, getting the rules right is tricky because dispute settlement is an extension of the rule of law into the international realm, and, at the same time, it is a practical measure aimed at creating a common institutional framework to smooth business transactions. Panels walk a fine line. Sometimes their decisions have significant legal consequences for national governments. Sometimes they are pragmatic compromises that allow disputants to craft a bilateral deal outside the WTO. The latter is frequently preferred to the former because it lessens the WTO's reach into behind-the-border policy areas. It is important also to remember that there is no legal or institutional basis for prioritizing one international legal venue over another. Pauwelyn (2001) argues persuasively that the absence of a hierarchy amongst international legal instruments allows governments to shop for the right tribunal that they think will give the best verdict. Nevertheless, it would seem that even as the WTO's Dispute Settlement Body does not always appear to limit the autonomy of member governments on its own, it does remain one of the most significant undertakings in the ongoing expansion of international rule making.

The fifth and final way that the WTO limits member autonomy is through the periodic review of national trade policies. The Trade Policy Review Mechanism (TPRM) was designed to enhance the transparency of trade policymaking. Many of the WTO's members are developing nations with few resources to spend on developing trade policy, let alone money to burn on publicizing legislation and producing reports for intergovernmental organizations (Drahos, 2005). And so the TPRM in theory serves a dual purpose. It increases the transparency of trade policy for members with few resources at the same time that its public pronouncements on a state's liberalization process serve as disciplinary measures to sanction and reward behaviour. In reality, the TPRM serves as something of a periodic reporting body, but its influence on members' actual patterns of trade policy has not been analysed.

FACT: *For better or worse, the multilateral trading system has become larger, more complicated, and, in some ways, less successful since the founding of the WTO.* When the WTO arrived late on the scene, it faced the formidable expectations of its supporters and the vociferous denunciations of a new brand of educated, highly informed, and politically engaged critic—the antiglobalization activist. The WTO became a target of an actively informed civil society because it was widely perceived to be secretive. The Uruguay Round affected more than 100 countries and created, overnight it seemed to many, a new international organization that would regulate a multitrillion-dollar flow of goods, services, and information to every corner of the globe.

In response, the WTO's supporters argued that it would increase the effectiveness of trade governance and would make the process of international economic integration more equitable and transparent. The GATT, it was frequently asserted, had resembled an exclusive club for rich countries (Howse, 2002). The WTO would democratize the use of trade for economic development. Today, the WTO more closely resembles a neighbourhood fitness facility than a country club. With 153 members, it has become a competitive environment in which the strong may dominate, but they no longer have the equipment all to themselves. This is the success of multilateralism, but it may also make the system less effective.

In an era of economic shift and political flux, the deadlock in agriculture negotiations exemplifies the minefield of complex and divergent interests that are paralysing the WTO. Agriculture negotiations are grouped around three important issues: the elimination of agricultural export subsidies permitted by developed countries, the reduction of domestic farm support (especially in the United States, Canada, Europe, and Japan), and the lowering of high agricultural tariffs designed to keep low-priced food products from developing countries out of northern markets (Turner, 2003). In a typical negotiating session, negotiators table a request for concessions and then make offers in response to other members' requests. The job of the negotiation chair is to help find a zone of agreement among the members. Working with the WTO Secretariat and its director-general, negotiators assist in the compilation of a final package to meet the minimum requirements of each participating member. Once a package is in place, negotiators review it and ask their governments whether the package on offer is better than the status quo (Bagwell & Staiger, 2006).

The process remains deadlocked because the developed countries have a huge political incentive to protect their rural producers. Farmers' votes are disproportionately weighty in many countries in the northern hemisphere because political systems have not evolved with the changing demographics of the wealthy, urban, northern hemisphere. For example, 80 per cent of Canada's population now lives in cities, whereas fewer than 60 per cent lived in cities 50 years ago. Today, representatives from rural ridings are elected by far fewer people than are representatives from cities, and they are subjected to the pressure of a small number of powerful, historically important interest groups. There remains a powerful constituency for agricultural protection in the United States, Canada, Japan, and Europe, and there is no indication that politicians will roll back farm support to any great extent in the near future. In fact, in the United States, subsidies for shrimp, corn, cotton, and rice increased during the presidential administration of George W. Bush.

Large industrializing countries, China and India in particular, also have an incentive to slow the agriculture negotiations. Trade liberalization is linked to structural adjustment and greater market efficiencies. China, for one, does not want a more efficient domestic agricultural sector just yet because it would swamp Chinese cities with peasants looking for work—a migratory process that China is attempting to manage and control. For India, the problem is more severe. There are 600 million Indian peasants eking out a living on small plots, and they constitute the vast majority of India's poor. The Indian agricultural sector is due for major reforms, but, until government develops a winning strategy to overcome the obstacles to structural adjustment, there can be no deal on agriculture.

A rising tide of international inequality and the failure of free trade to reduce poverty in significant and measurable ways in the poorest regions suggest that the theory at the heart of the international trading order may yet be called into question. The WTO's liberalization dynamic has been powered, until now, by the richest members, namely the United States and the European Union, but, at this point, developing countries make up three-quarters of the membership, and there is a corresponding shift in negotiating power towards new power brokers such as China and India. The stage is set for some significant changes in the upcoming decades. Whether the WTO will survive and thrive or capsize and sink under the weight of its own mandate is yet to be seen.

THE CANADIAN CONTEXT

In Canada, the debates about free trade raged throughout the 1980s. As is usually the case in trade debates, the biggest issue was political not economic. Nobody argued that Canada did not need foreign trade. Rather, the debate centred on the sort of trade that Canada could reasonably expect to engage in, given the historical realities of trade dependence with Britain and later with the United States. Would Canada's trade relations continue to be dominated by the United States, or would we develop a deeper engagement with the wider world economy? Continentalism is the idea that through the inevitable process of deeper economic integration, American business practices, political processes, social values, and economic ideas will increasingly influence Canada (Clarkson, 2002). Depending on one's worldview, continentalism is either a rising tide of Americanization, with the attendant loss of Canadian identity and autonomy, or it is a promised land of North American prosperity, in which Canadians finally share in the enormous bounty of US-style capitalism.

Canada's entry into a free trade agreement with the United States in 1989 provoked a new cycle of argument for and against integration that has continued with varying levels of fervour for 20 years. Today, intellectual support for continental integration waxes with the American business cycle. When times are good, the calls for deeper integration—perhaps even a common currency! — are loudest (Helleiner, 2006). When the American economy begins its inevitable descent into the trough of recession, Canadian pundits have a tendency to pat themselves on the back. Thanks to Canada's market model, peaks of market performance may not be as high, but the troughs are not as deep as those experienced south of the border. Continentalists were tellingly quiet as hundreds of thousands of Americans defaulted on their subprime mortgages and unregulated derivatives markets collapsed, bringing Wall Street to its knees in October 2008.

Canadians are remarkably comfortable with the concepts that accompany trade, including the expansion of international trade governance. In fact, Canadians show a significant tolerance for the expansion of international law, and for the intrusions into daily life, both large and small, that come along with it. There is some truth to the cliché that Americans organize their public values around the evocative reference in the Declaration of Independence to life, liberty, and the pursuit of happiness, but Canadians are more concerned about peace, order, and good government — the values enumerated in the chapeau of the British North America Act. It has long been considered conventional wisdom that Canadians are more differential to authority than are Americans, and this deference might account for some, but not all, of Canadians' tolerance for global governance.

In a nation dominated by brokerage politics and ruled for five of the past seven decades by a coalition of centrist interests known as the Liberal Party, overlapping sovereignties and governance from afar are part of the national psyche. Most Canadians remain comfortable with the concept of globalization if the resulting intergovernmental organizations direct attention to transnational "managerial" issues such as preventing climate change, stopping the spread of disease pandemics, or developing fair rules for trade and investment flows. As a result of this pragmatic attitude, "Canadians have been quite supportive of trade liberalization, and continue to be comfortable with even greater forms of integration, as long as the welfare objectives of the administrative state are maintained, and as long as globalization is not perceived to threaten valued objectives and Canadians' social values" (Wolfe & Mendelsohn, 2005, p. 60).

Powerful ideas about the efficacy of international trade played a large role in the creation of the WTO, and, not surprisingly, Canadian diplomats were at the centre of these plans for broader and deeper global governance. The standard view of Canadian participation at the WTO is that trade liberalization is a straightforward attempt to expand Canada's market access in North America and abroad in Europe, Latin America, Asia, and Africa. Extending market access is certainly one reason, but it is not a complete explanation for such a large investment in the multilateral trading system. A

Figure 1.2. *A Brief History of Canadian Trade Relations*

1815   Congress of Vienna ushers in a century of British hegemony.
      Corn Laws create preferences for Canadian wheat in Britain

1846   Britain repeals the Corn Laws

1854   Governor General Lord Elgin negotiates the Elgin-Marcy
      Reciprocity Treaty between the United States and the
      Canadian colonies, creating another preferential market for
      colonial goods

1866   In retaliation for British support for the Confederacy in the
      Civil War, the United States ends reciprocity

1932   Britain retreats from almost a century of unilateral free trade
      and creates a system of preferences for Commonwealth
      dominions

1935   Canada and the United States sign the Reciprocal Trade
      Agreements Act, establishing freer trade than ever before

1941   President Roosevelt and Prime Minister Churchill sign the
      Atlantic Charter, laying a foundation for postwar economic
      institutions based upon the principle of non-discrimination

1944   Charters for the International Monetary Fund, International
      Bank for Reconstruction and Development (World Bank),
      and the International Trade Organization (GATT) are nego-
      tiated at Bretton Woods, New Hampshire

1947–1948   Canada and the United States initiate but do not conclude a
      new free trade agreement

1948   The GATT comes into force in Canada, Britain, the United
      States and five other countries

1965   The Auto Pact is signed between the United States and Canada

1989   The Canada–United States Free Trade Agreement (CUSFTA) is
      signed

1994   CUSFTA is enlarged to include Mexico and becomes the North
      American Free Trade Agreement (NAFTA)

1995   The World Trade Organization is born

1996   Canada signs free trade agreements with Chile and Israel

2001   The first trade round since the birth of the WTO is launched at
      Doha, Qatar

2002   Canada–Costa Rica Free Trade Agreement is signed

2006   Canada's decades-long softwood lumber battle with the United
      States results in quantitative lumber restrictions imposed on
      Canadian lumber producers for the third time

2008   Canada signs free trade agreements with Peru and the European
      Free Trade Association (Iceland, Liechtenstein, Norway, and
      Switzerland)

better explanation highlights the way that Canada's engagement at the international level is part of an historical growth and development strategy. Over the past several decades, Canadian trade and industrial policies have been developed on the basis of a number of assumptions, including the following:

- Multilateral participation helps Canada diversify its export markets (Dymond & Hart, 2004);
- Multilateralism can be used to defend a nation's current model of social provision against the forces of continental integration (Lammert, 2004);
- Trade agreements counterbalance Canada's unequal relationship with the United States, to a certain extent, and protect Canadian commercial interests (Schwanen, 1997);
- Participation in international organizations enhances Canada's international influence — a worthwhile endeavour with little impact on government's ability to make public policy (Inwood, 2005).

How well do these assumptions bear up under a sustained scrutiny of Canadian participation at the WTO? The case studies show that, despite the potentially contradictory nature of these assumptions, WTO participation does a relatively good job of addressing and perhaps even fulfilling at least some of these goals some of the time. Nevertheless, the sheer size and scope of WTO governance makes forward momentum difficult. Therefore, the largest member countries that have been big investors in trade multilateralism have subsequently diversified into a large number of regional and bilateral arrangements. For example, both the United States and the European Union actively pursue formalized trade ties outside the WTO, and both have concluded a number of important deals over the past decade. In Latin America, the Treaty Establishing a Common Market between the Argentine Republic, the Federative Republic of Brazil, the Republic of Paraguay, and the Eastern Republic of Uruguay, better known as the Treaty of Asunción or the treaty creating the Mercado Común del Sur (Mercosur), predates the WTO but has recently expanded to include associate status for Bolivia, Chile, Colombia, Ecuador, and Peru. In 2006, the membership created a Mercosur parliament to smooth the settlement of disputes and to provide a consultative voice on infrastructure and development projects. Outside of NAFTA, Canada has little investment in bilateral dealmaking, having concluded bilateral trade agreements with just four partners: Israel, Chile, Costa Rica, and Peru.[6]

The simple truth of the matter is that the United States accounts for four-fifths of Canada's trade. Because the US economy is so large compared to Canada's, and political pressure from American interests so intense at times,

Canada prefers to use neutral institutions to manage the trade relationship. The biggest problem that Canada faces in this regard is that Canada is not America. Canadian producers compete directly with their American counterparts in a number of lucrative domestic markets. The Canadian industrial model is significantly different from that of the United States — in everything from stumpage fees to securities regulation — so American lawmakers are often left scratching their heads while their constituents rage about unfair trading practices. In general, these charges usually add up to competitive stresses and regulatory frictions. But when so much of Canada's trade flows to the United States, one must not discount the seriousness of lobbyist provocations.

For American interest groups that pressure their government to get tough with Canadian producers, there is a simple solution to regulatory friction. Canada and the United States should harmonize their regulatory institutions (Young, 2000). Canadian policymakers are usually wary of this argument for a very good reason; it is most often assumed that Canada would adopt an American approach to market regulation. This assumption in turn raises a provocative question: why shouldn't Canada harmonize its regulations with the world's largest and most successful free market institutions? Of course, in some cases regulatory harmonization is in the best interest of both countries. Take for example the Great Lakes Basin Compact among the eight states that border the continent's largest bodies of fresh water. They have adopted a sweeping plan to ban the diversion of water out of the Great Lakes' natural basin. Ontario and Quebec have already passed similar legislation. This is a significant environmental issue that may require joint monitoring in the future, and both countries have a long history of cooperating on issues such as this.

In matters of trade, however, Canada has an enviable position as a key partner with the world's wealthiest country while at the same time remaining a discrete distance from the volatile American business cycle. This position has been preserved by maintaining a certain distance between Canadian and American economic and monetary policy. Canada is therefore less concerned about the loss of political autonomy that comes along with WTO governance than about the possibility of using WTO mechanisms to preserve policy space within the context of Canada–US trade relations. However, just because Canadian policymakers are not seemingly concerned about the disciplinary effect of WTO governance does not mean that they shouldn't be. By ignoring the potential issues that arise from the unforeseen consequences of WTO governance, Canada increases the possibility that the strategy could backfire, leaving government with less policy autonomy and very little leverage in the Canada–US relationship.

Between 1995 and 2005, Canada increased export trade by 252 per cent, the greatest increase in the G8 (Marshall, 2005). However, the threat of deeper dependence has not come from expansionist American industrialists in recent years. The greatest irony is that increasing demand for Canada's exports has become the greatest threat to economic independence. The most important challenge faced by Canada's policymakers today has to do with the difficult task of managing Canada's trade relationships within bullish, unstable commodity markets. In the first decade of the twenty-first century, Canadian industrial policy is facing a challenge that everyone thought had been addressed after the stagflation of the 1970s. Once again, the loony is following commodity prices, and Canadian exporters are more dependent upon natural resource markets than ever. Consider some of Canada's resource-export rankings collected recently by economists at the Toronto Dominion Bank (Burleton & Apollonova, 2006). Canada has the fourth largest endowment of natural resources on the planet. We are the world's third largest producer of natural gas and the seventh largest oil producer. We are the number one producer of potash and uranium, the third largest producer of diamonds, the fifth largest producer of platinum, and the seventh largest producer of gold. Canada is also the world's largest producer of forest products. Most of these resources are extracted and sent to the United States. NAFTA accounts for 80 per cent of Canada's total exports, a trade flow that has grown by 250 per cent since 1989.[7]

Commentators on current industrial policies, such as Jim Stanford, chief economist for the Canadian Auto Workers union, point out that Canada's staples boom could end badly for two reasons. First, it ties the Canadian job market to commodity prices. Many of Canada's exports are unfinished goods destined for other jurisdictions where they are factors in the production of high value-added goods, which have wider profit margins (Stanford, 2007). Canadian industry's reliance on staples exports means lower margins on traded goods. Furthermore, high value-added exports are a more stable source of domestic output and jobs (Cross & Ghanem, 2005). High value-added manufacturing creates employment, facilitates industrial specialization, and remains the most reliable driver of GDP growth—all necessary ingredients for stable, long-term economic development. By passing on the opportunity to develop high value-added manufacturing on this side of the border, policymakers doom Canadian workers to riding the waves of commodity prices. When times are good, this is not a problem. But when resource prices fall, jobs are lost and entire regions of the country can slide into recession. Albertans have long ridden the ups and downs of oil prices. Likewise, Canadians on the east coast were caught unprepared for the collapse of cod stocks in the 1980s—the repercussions of which are still felt today.

Not surprisingly, trade litigation has been a mixed bag for Canada. Over 95 per cent of Canadian trade with the United States is dispute free, but significant issue areas remain: softwood lumber, live swine, and wheat are three such areas. In the first ten years of the WTO, Canada completed 20 panels, the biggest participant in dispute settlement after the European Union and the United States. One concern highlighted by the case studies that follow is that Canada would benefit from a bolder trade policy in which trade diversification, development, cultural priorities, and human security are pursued as joint objectives rather than discrete goals. When it comes to trade, the Canadian focus is too often on questions of what the United States wants and on what strengthens Canada's position in North American markets.

Some trade watchers may be tempted to suggest that Canada is a big trader with a small trader mentality, in other words, that Canadian policy focuses too much on maintaining the favour of Canada's main trading partner and not enough on developing an independent strategy for trade diversification and industrial competitiveness. I would not disagree, but I would add that Canadian participation raises the issue of competing national priorities because WTO membership involves political commitment to a particular governance model. Even as trade liberalization offers new economic options to Canadian producers, it often requires that the government give priority to market access commitments over public goods provision.

The effects of this new governance model will not be seen right away, but we do know that the impacts of trade liberalization vary depending on a number of factors, including a country's wealth, level of development, and the type of regulatory mechanisms employed to manage the relationship between markets and the public domain (Hall & Soskice, 2001). The past 20 years of liberalization have not sounded the death knell for the Canadian state, nor has Canada's economy become an appendage of the US economy. Canadian industry may not be as diversified as many economists would like to see, but Canada is also not quite the "branch plant" society that George Grant (1965) envisioned more than four decades ago.

What then have the past decades, particularly the years since 1995, taught us about the relationship between Canada and the global economy? Recent research emphasizes three broadly significant insights for scholars and Canadian policymakers. First, political institutions are as important as markets for the organization of trade relations (Hall & Soskice, 2001). Second, national sovereignty is not a necessary casualty of global governance (Drache, 2004). Third, the realist strand of international relations theory that emphasizes power considerations over all other factors has been subject to serious criticism and has proven to be increasingly difficult to maintain in a complex and interdependent world system (Keohane & Milner, 1996).

Diverse scholars from Sylvia Ostry to Robert Cox have demonstrated that such a narrow focus misses the big picture of global flux.

In theory, these three insights are unsurprising truisms; obviously, governments play a big role in the globalization dynamic, and everybody knows that analyses of causation that focus on a narrow band of factors seldom prove much at all. Nevertheless, sometimes the most obvious insights are the most astute. With that in mind, we can sum up the lessons learned by saying that a circumscribed loss of policy autonomy is often a very real by-product of deeper economic integration, but a line must be drawn between perceived and actual constraint. Current forms of multilateral trade governance may sometimes widen the gap between international goals and domestic priorities, but scholars and policymakers must not magnify the perception that states and national economies are a necessary casualty of deeper economic integration.

A NEW WAY TO STUDY DISPUTE SETTLEMENT

Scholars who study the WTO are generally drawn from several disciplines, including business, political science, economics, and law. Most are informed by a broad and multidisciplinary literature that analyses the WTO in terms of its relationship to business interests, civil society, states, and other international organizations. Out of necessity, our analysis will shift from time to time between the national and international levels. Diplomatic mandates and economic activity are rooted at the state level, but negotiation and dispute settlement happen at the international level. The levels-of-analysis problem is unavoidable when examining processes and responsibilities that have been the sovereign prerogative of states in the past but are now part of international relations.

Many Organization for Economic Co-operation and Development (OECD) governments in the period after World War II wisely developed a foreign policy strategy that pursued a number of overlapping and complimentary goals, such as development, diplomacy, security, and trade objectives—all of which are considered to have broad international benefits. Nevertheless, during the heyday of deregulation in the early 1990s, many international experts— from scholars to journalists and business professionals—imagined that the market, not governments, would set the pace and agenda of globalization. In this view, the emerging world trading order would become the driving force behind deeper global integration. They believed that the WTO would become a central organizing institution, presiding over a host of issues and governance areas that come into contact with the global marketplace.

The WTO was theorized at the centre of a web of "trade and" issues, such as trade and the environment, and trade and public health, which were linked to a progressive program of trade liberalization by virtue of the fact that they represented regulatory areas within which new trade disciplines were likely to replace older national policies (see Figure 1.3). However, very few of these issues are currently on the negotiating table, and, although issues such as government procurement and foreign investment are earmarked for future attention, it seems unlikely that others such as labour standards and environmental regulation will be explicitly linked to trade liberalization in the future.

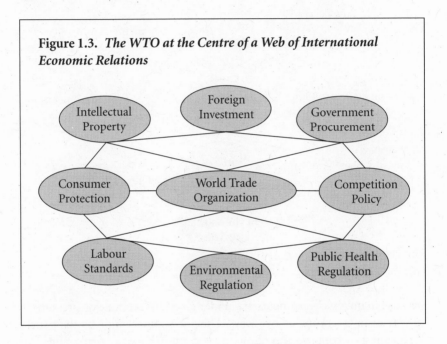

Figure 1.3. *The WTO at the Centre of a Web of International Economic Relations*

Trade scholars now realize that the web of international economic relations is more complex and state-oriented than originally thought. Domestic authority is once more recognized as the primary shaper of international affairs (Wendt, 1992). It is clear that the position of the WTO in the international economic order is changing: it is evolving away from an expansive mandate, which made it a quasi-constitutional and centralizing institution and regrouping around its core competencies, which are dispute settlement and tariff reduction (see Figure 1.4). The result is likely to be more focused trade adjudication and an agenda-setting body that is not a constitutional keystone for the global economic order but rather a single node within a network of international legal and economic institutions in which the state remains a significant anchor-point.

The WTO is the first worldwide, multilateral "commercial court" whose members have decided to always abide by its rulings (Krikorian, 2005). The "binding" quality of WTO dispute settlement makes it more effective

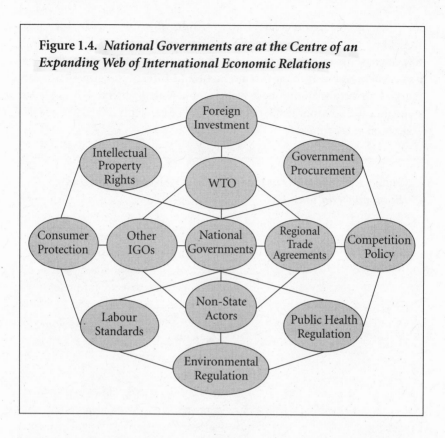

Figure 1.4. *National Governments are at the Centre of an Expanding Web of International Economic Relations*

because member governments are under a certain amount of pressure to resolve disputes in one of two ways. They may either abide by the panel's final ruling or come to some sort of bilateral negotiated agreement. Not every case goes all the way to a final panel ruling. Many are resolved prior to this stage. Likewise, some cases drag on for a long time after the panel presents its findings, as disputants appeal certain aspects of the ruling, file compliance complaints, and, in some cases, even decide to pay monetary penalties rather than bring domestic practices into line with international agreement. Perhaps a case study approach is the best way to examine these many different situations systematically.

Case studies have been described by one researcher as "analytical narratives" (Alston, 2005). In one sense, they should also give enough information that scholars who wish to draw their own conclusions from the evidence given may do so. But they are also narratives or factual stories about international law. Those who engage with these cases may find that they begin to develop an ear for the give and take of international economic relations. More importantly, they will learn how to develop multidisciplinary frames with which to collect information, assess its significance, and understand how it relates to the other diverse bodies of empirical information used to analyse international economic relations.

A case study method is useful for analysing dispute settlement because it allows the student of international trade to analyse the many different ways that interests and actors cluster around an issue area. I use a heuristic tool that social scientists call "process tracing." It involves examining actor behaviour and comparing its outcomes across different cases. In this case study approach, the WTO panel process remains an independent variable, and the dependent variable, the variable that we have isolated for study, is Canadian public policy. This approach requires a rigorous analysis of dispute panel texts and then a second "process tracing" step that examines changes in policy following the dispute. It raises the question of whose behaviour matters? To frame the question in social scientific terms, we would ask, what are the intervening variables between dispute settlement and Canadian public policy? Business interests at home, lobby groups in the complaining country, and governmental and non-governmental policy advocates are just a few of the many interested groups, or variables, that must be considered.

Even so, the question remains, how do we decide which variables are important? We need a template that helps us to sort through the thorny issues of cooperation, conflict, negotiation, and compromise that bind all actors — be they firms, governments, activists, or panellists — into what Susan Strange (1988) has termed a "network of bargains." She means that international actors (e.g., governments, firms, non-governmental organizations, or other types of purposeful groups) are caught up in a system of interaction in which they have a range of "feasible choices" that depend, to a great extent, on the choices made by other actors (Strange 1988, p. 39).

Susan Strange was one of those old-fashioned political economists who believed that the fads (her term, not mine) of political science, from hegemonic stability theory through regime theory and institutionalist theory, did not add up to a hill of beans. In her view, good scholarship was predicated upon a sceptical view of perceived wisdom and a solid understanding of the way that the rules of the game and the key players shaped outcomes in the global economy. She argued that scholars of international political economy need a way to "synthesize politics and economics by means of a structural analysis of the effects of states — or more properly any kind of political authority — on markets and, conversely of market forces on states" (Strange, 1988, pp. 13–14). This conceptualization relies to a great extent on a structuralist understanding of the international realm, which means that it is an understanding of international political economy (IPE) that places primary importance on the ways in which the system itself shapes policies and priorities.

Strange argues that most IPE specialists study the relational aspects of power — the power of states and economic actors in comparison to that of other states and economic actors. This approach only takes our understanding of power so far. It tells us how power can be used to accumulate wealth and prestige vis-à-vis other players of the international game. We also need to understand the way that power can be used to set the rules of the game. "[In] the competitive games now being played out in the world system between states and between economic enterprises, it is increasingly structural power that counts far more than relational power" (Strange, 1988, p. 24). The network of bargains is not a static or monolithic construction. In fact, powerful actors have the ability to make and change the rules of the game — essentially tilting the playing field in their favour. The network of bargains is a set of relationships embedded within the structural context of the global political economy.

How can we use this concept of a network of bargains that is rooted in the structural power of states and markets to understand the impact of dispute settlement on Canadian public policy? Strange gives the following advice: "You should look for the key bargains in any situation, and then decide which might, and which probably will not, be liable to change, altering the range of choices for all or some of those concerned" (Strange 1988, p. 39). In essence, the network of bargains approach examines a number of relationships in which different groups stand to win or lose. For example, there is the relationship between the economic actor, which is almost always a multinational corporation, and the member government that will take the dispute to the WTO. Litigation is expensive, and governments decide which cases they will prosecute at the WTO and which they will not. The relationship between firm and government is therefore an important one, as we will discover when we examine the Bombardier case in Chapter 4.

Second, there is the relationship between member governments. The density of trade and diplomatic ties are significant variables in the successful resolution of disputes. Where trade flows are sparse, there is little leverage for trade retaliation if the panel decision is not acceptable to the respondent, making resolution more difficult. Third, there is the relationship between the WTO and its member governments. Do some governments have more confidence that their cases are winnable? Is this because of the legality of particular cases or because they are skilled at moving the levers of litigation? This variable could also be described as the relationship between member governments and the trade governance environment. Some governments are more confident and skilled at multilateral economic diplomacy than others. This skill and confidence are frequently functions of wealth and information, as I discussed above.

Fourth, there is the relationship between market actors and the WTO. Technically, firms have no legal standing at the WTO, but they certainly have opinions about the efficacy of WTO dispute settlement. Does dispute settlement make it easier to do business in the global marketplace? For some firms, the benefits of dispute settlement may be few and far between. For example, in the controversial area of intellectual property rights enforcement, the Agreement on Trade-Related Aspects of Intellectual Property Rights ought to be a bulwark against information theft, but, in reality, dispute settlement has done little to stem the global torrent of pirated information, from music to films, video games, and industrial secrets.

Finally, there is the relationship between member governments and their citizens. Citizens are both market actors and members of a political community. Because the WTO's mechanisms are not commanded by democratically elected officials, their influence on public policy is frequently controversial. It is the job of governments to use WTO mechanisms judiciously, with an eye to constituent interests certainly but also with an eye on the big picture—the long-term costs and benefits for national community. It is the job of citizens to hold government accountable for action in the international realm and to elect representatives that are able to navigate between domestic and international levels adequately—to negotiate what Putnam (1988) has termed "the two-level game." In this regard, the relationship between states and citizens is one in which the WTO plays no formal role, but its presence is nevertheless constantly felt in small and large ways.

Of course, there are other emerging bargaining relationships that are already starting to affect the study of international political economy (IPE). For example, there is the relationship between citizens and firms that takes the form of corporate social responsibility charters and other guarantees that labour rights will be respected even when governments cannot enforce them. It should also be noted that not all of these relationships involve formal bargaining processes per se. For example, the relationship between the WTO and member governments ought not to be read in these terms because there is no formal bargaining process around dispute settlement that involves member governments and the WTO—unless we raise the question of conflict of interest or influence peddling. In that regard, one of the WTO's singular achievements has been a lack of political corruption.

Nevertheless, most of the other relationships I have described do involve some form of formal or informal negotiation, between the parties or within one of the parties involved. It is this process of cooperation and conflict, winning and losing, that contributes to policy change. There is a downside to this approach: a single actor or institution seldom holds a smoking gun. It may be impossible to determine exactly which variable caused a policy to change, but at least we have a solid understanding of the mix of variables, the accumulation of winners and losers, that likely tipped the scales in favour of a new policy strategy.

This case study method seems unwieldy. At best, it appears to deal with too many variables to make much sense out of any situation. At worst, it carries within it the danger of being so informal as to appear journalistic rather than scholarly. (Interestingly, Susan Strange did not really want to be a scholar. Given her choice, she would have chosen a career in journalism.) So how do we render the network of bargains useful? First, not all relationships are relevant all the time, so we need to focus on areas where bargaining is taking place. Second, we need a template into which we can feed the appropriate information. Without a map on which to fix coordinates, the relationships we examine will not always make much sense. Therefore, I propose that we divide each study into a number of sections, which has the advantage of allowing us to identify, define, and distinguish between different economic, legal, and political relationships within the network of bargains. To that end, each case study will be organized in the following way.

The first part of each case study sets out the relevant legal and economic concepts that relate to the case at hand. The second section describes the dispute itself, paying special attention to the arguments put forward by all parties and the reasoning by which the panel delivered its decision. Most cases taken to the WTO are appealed, so the actions of the WTO Appellate Body will also be discussed. The third section describes and analyses the post-dispute policy environment and examines the implications of the case for Canadian public policy. In many cases, the findings of dispute settlement panels require that Canada change legislation, or at the very least alter governmental policies, in order to come into line with the panel's interpretation of treaty obligations. These changes, even when they seem insignificant, have important implications for the future of public policy.

Many groups are interested in how Canada responds to dispute settlement. Some want to see all the proposed changes implemented. Others wish to see the status quo maintained, even at the expense of noncompliance. Of course, all actors are interested in the bottom line — how will a government's policy changes affect markets for goods and services? There are numerous relationships within the network of bargains. I will look at the many different bargains struck and weigh their effect on policy change. In this way, the following five cases may act as satellites in a sort of global positioning system with which we can chart Canada's course through the waters of global trade politics.

Notes

1. Farmers are the most common example. In the global north (northern hemisphere), farmers benefit from many state subsidies, and, arguably, they command a louder voice in national politics because rural ridings have fewer voters than urban ridings. Further, farmers have an interest in maintaining protectionist trade policies because international markets for agricultural goods are notoriously prone to price fluctuations. As small- and medium-sized business owners, farmers know that a year or two of low prices, combined with a little bad luck and low levels of government support, can destroy a family business.

2. The non-discrimination model is preferable to a deeper regulatory approach because it strikes a balance between disciplining protectionist interests and undermining the sovereign will of national publics. See McGinnis and Movsesian (2000, p. 518).

3. The WTO's approach to disciplining protectionism also resembles Madisonian jurisprudence to the extent that certain agreements use procedure-oriented tests to establish fair standards for trade openness. Universal standards are less likely to be captured by special interests. See James Madison (1787). See also McGinnis and Movsesian (2000, p. 519).

4. The World Intellectual Property Organization manages the Collection of Laws for Electronic Access (CLEA), which provides electronic copies of intellectual property legislation from over 100 countries. It can be accessed at www.wipo.int/clea/en/ index.jsp.

5. The trade rounds were as follows: Geneva (1947) sees 23 member countries participate, and GATT enters into force; Annecy (1949) sees 13 member countries participate; Torquay (1950–1951) has 38 countries as participants — these early rounds created the norms and practices that underpin trade negotiation today; Geneva (1955–1956), with 26 countries, sees deeper tariff cuts and the development of strategy for developing country participation; Dillon (1960–1961), with 26 countries, continues tariff reductions; Kennedy (1963–1967), with 62 countries, sees the first anti-dumping agreement; Tokyo (1973–1979) has 102 members and sees product-by-product tariff reduction and improvements to the GATT system (i.e., dispute settlement process established); Uruguay (1986–1994), with 125 countries, reduces subsidies and quotas, creates the WTO, and regulates intellectual property; Doha (2001–present), with 146–149 members, is focussing on development, agricultural support, and industrial subsidies. However, this latest round of trade negotiations was suspended between July 2006 and January 2007, and there was only fitful progress made upon resumption of talks. The Singapore issues — investment, competition policy, government procurement, and transparency — are off the table for this round. For an in-depth discussion of the history of the GATT, see Trebilcock and Howse (1999).

6. What exactly does Canada trade with Costa Rica? Predictably, the value of Canadian exports to Costa Rica is not very great. Canada–Costa Rica trade only accounted for about C$81 million dollars in 2007. (In comparison, Canada's total exports for 2007 were worth more than C$450 billion.) But that trade is spread out over many different industries. These include everything from frozen-food manufacturing to paper mills and pharmaceuticals. Surprisingly, 21 of the top 25 industries in Canada increased their trade with Costa Rica since 2002. It seems clear that trade diversification is possible if government has the political will to pursue deals that extend Canada's economic relations beyond North America. Unquestionably, the WTO is part of the equation, although the extent to which it facilitates trade diversification is still unclear. As I have argued in the previous chapter, the WTO is a large and not very nimble organization that has been a somewhat effective agent of stability for international trade — especially vis-à-vis dispute settlement. But it may not be the best place to pursue a diversification strategy.

7. Canada has a huge American market for minerals, agricultural products, and softwood lumber. But energy is our least diversified export — 95 per cent of all energy exports go to the United States (Sydor, 2003). Also not surprising is the fact that, in 2005, energy was Canada's top export, accounting for 80 per cent of our trade surplus. Canada exports mostly oil and natural gas, each of which earned more than C$30 billion in 2005, but coal exports to Asia are also up (Roy, 2006). Contrary to the Macdonald Commission's optimistic predictions, Cross and Ghanem (2005) estimate that natural resource products account for 60 per cent of exports, up several percentage points from twenty years ago.

CHAPTER TWO

Subsidies and Countervailing Measures: The Case of Softwood Lumber

Two movements have featured prominently in the recent history of global markets. The first is a limited diversification of internal markets with broad and shallow benefits for consumers. Prices for consumer goods have stayed steady and, in some cases, declined. At the same time, consumers in developed countries have never had more products to choose from. The second dynamic is an increase in intra-sectoral competition that is frequently accompanied by friction at the interface between national regulatory systems. Having more products to choose from benefits consumers, but it means more competitors for manufacturers. One of the WTO's central functions is the adjudication of disputes that develop at these friction points among trade partners. For the past decade, contingent protection measures such as anti-dumping remedies and countervailing duties have been the preferred non-tariff barriers used by embattled domestic producers in North America. The Canada–United States softwood lumber dispute provides a timely and highly illustrative example of the evolving nature of trade remedy action under the WTO system.

These dynamics of diversification and competition raise two questions that are of central importance throughout this chapter. First, what does the use of contingent protection measures mean for Canada's approach to regulating industry? Anti-dumping and countervailing legislation has created a new order of trade conflict at a time when intra-sectoral competition has increased state support in a number of sectors. Second, how do interest group politics come to bear in this dispute? Anti-dumping actions are difficult to counter through multilateral mechanisms because, in the absence of international competition standards, trade remedies are an increasingly important feature of industrial policy. They effectively blur the distinction between national competition strategies and non-tariff protectionism (Gagné, 2003). In the softwood case, dispute settlement was not effective because Canada, as the smaller economy, faced the challenge of defending its regulatory practices against the entrenched interests of a much larger trading partner.

The first section of this case study examines the use of anti-dumping measures in the context of international economic relations, paying particular attention to current trade tensions around softwood lumber. Thanks in no small part to GATT-based tariff reductions, anti-dumping regimes and other non-tariff trade barriers have been used to a greater extent in both developed and developing nations. Dumping is the single largest competition issue currently facing the international trade regime, and, in the first ten years of dispute settlement, anti-dumping and subsidies cases were the most litigated disputes.

The second section examines Canada's softwood cases at the NAFTA Secretariat and the WTO. Much to the dismay of its NAFTA partners, the US Department of Commerce has been especially aggressive in the protection of domestic industry through countervailing duties and anti-dumping litigation. Canada has concluded 11 legal challenges of American anti-dumping duties—4 at the NAFTA Secretariat and 7 at the WTO. Canada and the United States regulate their forestry industries in very different ways. Despite a high degree of corporate integration in the North American forestry industry, Canada has persisted in maintaining a unique regulatory model designed to address environmental and employment issues in provinces that are economically dependent upon the forestry industry (Ciuriak, 2005).

The final section analyses the outcome of these panel decisions and the negotiated settlement that recently ended this round of the softwood lumber trade war. Voluntary export restraints and other bilateral mechanisms for managing, rather than liberalizing, softwood trade have been the most popular methods for handling the friction that arises from the interface between different regulatory models. Canadian policymakers originally hoped that litigation would force a better export deal for softwood producers. They preferred a settlement in which, at the very least, the United States lowered its duties and returned all of the duties collected since 2001. The American industry and its powerful lumber lobby in Congress wanted a settlement that would limit the flow of cheap Canadian lumber into the US market and allow forestry companies to keep all or most of the US$5 billion in duties collected and disbursed under government regulations at that time, known as the "Byrd Amendment."

The current arrangement, much like the Softwood Lumber Agreement of 1996, is a second-best outcome to an intractable dispute. Canadian policy-makers are now aware that the WTO's dispute settlement architecture is not always very effective in bilateral disputes with the United States. They need to incorporate this knowledge into future litigation and compliance induce-ment strategies. One of the aims of dispute settlement is to bring both sides together in a negotiated settlement. But when one side is so much more eco-nomically powerful than the other, there is often the perception of an unfair advantage in bilateral negotiation. An old adage goes something like this: a successful negotiation is one in which both sides leave the table a little unhappy. The Harper government put a brave face on the most recent nego-tiated settlement, but nobody on the Canadian side of the border was con-vinced that it was a great deal. Were American interests similarly dissatisfied with the outcome? I suspect that the Americans were dissatisfied, although perhaps not to the same extent as the Canadians. It must have been a suc-cessful negotiation!

The conclusion briefly examines the softwood lumber issue from the perspective of other interested groups within the extensive network of bar-gains. I briefly consider the interests of American retailers, American home-owners, Canadian environmentalists, and Canada's First Nations. The easy generalities of the "Canadian side" and the "American side" break down under closer examination. This analysis does not discount the structural imbalances in the Canada–US trade relationship, but it does offer a chance to think about the many ramifications of continental trade flows and the ways in which interests don't necessarily fall into discrete national boxes.

CONTINGENT PROTECTION MEASURES AND WTO GOVERNANCE

Dumping is the practice of exporting a product for less than the cost of pro-ducing it or for less than the "normal value" of the product within the firm's home market. Dumping is a popular way to reduce a glut in one's own mar-ket, and agricultural goods are sometimes treated this way. Canadian dairy producers have been taken to the WTO for this practice. Dumping is also a useful way to gain access to a foreign market dominated by other firms. Chi-nese goods are often hit with anti-dumping duties because they are priced much lower than similar goods produced in nations where the cost of labour is higher. In economic terms, dumping is a rational, profit-maximiz-ing action, with little or no harm to global welfare (Mankiw & Swagel, 2005).

In many cases, dumping goods on foreign markets can even improve consumer welfare by lowering prices. In the domestic market, producers sometimes sell their goods below cost in an effort to clear inventory or break into a market dominated by rival producers. In international trade, where countries have very different factor endowments, selling goods for less than the cost of production is largely considered to be an unfair form of competition.

The WTO regulates the use of anti-dumping measures through the Agreement on Implementation of Article VI of the GATT 1994, also known as the Anti-Dumping Agreement (AD), and it regulates countervailing duties through the Agreement on Subsidies and Countervailing Measures (SCM). Following World War II, Article VI of the GATT provided for the right of contracting parties to apply anti-dumping measures. At the end of the Uruguay Round, more detailed rules for the application of such measures were spelled out in the Anti-Dumping Agreement.[1] A companion to the AD, the SCM is intended to delineate acceptable forms of state support from unfair subsidy practices. In litigation that involves the agreements, the trend has been towards the creation of a higher standard of proof in recent years. This attempt to dam the tide of injury actions notified to the WTO each year has not been entirely successful.[2] Members continue to enact anti-dumping legislation because they've noted its effective use by European and North American governments to protect domestic producers (Mankiw & Swagel, 2005).

The United States, in particular, uses anti-dumping legislation to attack a wide range of pricing practices in an attempt to enforce a more rigorous standard on the use of state support. Many of the large developing nations who implemented the Tokyo Round tariff reductions have also begun to equip themselves with anti-dumping legislation. Ruggie (1994) reminds trade watchers that the goals of trade liberalization have never been literally free trade. Rather, they have been to move from the strictures of managed trade to a more liberal and multilateral governance model. Nevertheless, it is precisely the expanding membership of the WTO that has facilitated a shift on the part of many members towards the use of ad hoc, non-tariff measures to shelter their domestic producers because along with accession comes the right to institutionalize anti-dumping statutes (Drope & Hansen, 2006).

Dumping becomes a public policy issue when jobs, growth, and national competitiveness are undercut by the profit-maximizing behaviour of foreign firms. Empirical evidence supports this hypothesis. Bourgeois and Messerlin (1998) examined European anti-dumping cases between 1980 and 1997. They found an inverse relationship between the height of the tariff wall protecting domestic firms and the frequency of their involvement in anti-dumping cases. As tariffs fell, countries engaged more frequently in anti-dumping trade remedy actions. Conventional wisdom, which says that anti-dumping trade remedies are designed to combat the anticompetitive practices of exporters, misses the main thrust of these laws — protecting strategic industries from the predations of low-priced foreign imports. Governments rely on aggressive litigation strategies to shelter industries faced with competitive pressure to cut costs up and down the production chain. Nevertheless, as Anderson (2003) argues, trade remedy action in the softwood context is necessarily central to the compromise of embedded liberalism because Canada and the United States have structured their respective forest products industries in different ways.

Canada maintains a strong state presence in the forestry industry, owning forest lands and setting the cost of cutting on these lands. This is not necessarily the case in all provinces, of course. In Atlantic Canada, a market-driven system tied to private ownership of timber lots is the norm, and in British Columbia, there has been movement towards a market-based stumpage formula. Yet the vast majority of Canadian timber is harvested on Crown land, which gives the perception of government interference in timber markets. In Canada, the use of Crown resources to organize markets has a long history. The American compromise with embedded liberalism consists of generous trade remedy measures that offset the relatively higher cost of cutting on privately owned timber reserves. National institutions shape the trade advantages of domestic firms in very different ways. The biggest unintended outcome of the dispute settlement system has been the attempt by domestic producers and national governments to use the uncomfortable fit between national regulatory systems as a pretext for foot-dragging, pre-emptive litigation, and other political roadblocks designed to avoid compliance.

THE SOFTWOOD LUMBER DISPUTE

Trade experts trace the current lumber battle between Canada and the United States back to the early 1980s, although disagreements over lumber date back as far as the nineteenth century. The dispute revolves around the methods used to sell trees to timber producers. In the United States, many timber harvesters buy trees from the owners of timber lots. Harvesters hold contracts for cutting on dozens or, in the cases of the largest multinationals, thousands of lots. Sixty per cent of timberland is privately owned. In the case of government-owned timberland (approximately 40 per cent of timberland), harvesting rights are auctioned to the highest bidder. The cost of maintaining timber stands and various other environmental and administrative costs are borne by the lot owners, who in turn pass them on to timber purchasers.

In the Canadian regulatory model, the timber firm does not purchase trees from the private sector. Rather, firms purchase the right to harvest trees from a provincial government. Stumpage fees are set by the provincial government and reflect the cost of maintaining forest land. These funds pay for some environmental and social programs, but, of course, the crux of the matter for US timber producers is the prominent provincial involvement in the Canadian industry. Stumpage fees are adjusted periodically, four times a year in British Columbia, for example, and, although adjustment may enable fees to reflect the up-to-the-minute value of Canadian timber, it also allows regulators to compensate for other costs in the industry. Low stumpage fees are one way provincial governments protect rural wages and jobs (Haggart, 2005). As a result, the cost of harvesting timber in Canada is lower than in the United States.

The first round of the softwood lumber dispute began in 1982 and ended in a win for Canada at the US Department of Commerce (DOC). The US industry petitioned against Canadian softwood lumber imports, arguing that under US countervailing duty law, Canadian stumpage fees were subsidies for lumber exporters. By May of the next year, the DOC concluded that stumpage did not confer a countervailable subsidy. In 1986, American timber lobbyists reactivated their petition for countervailing duties using a federal court case from the year before (a dispute over imports from Mexico) as a favourable precedent. After preliminary investigation, the DOC found that Canadian stumpage fees conferred a subsidy of approximately 15 per cent on producers. Canada signed a memorandum of understanding (MOU) agreeing to place a 15 per cent export duty on lumber shipped to the United States. The MOU remained in effect until 1991.

Canada terminated the MOU, believing that it had a solid case for the new Canada–US Free Trade Agreement's Chapter 19 dispute settlement mechanism. This touched off the third round of trade conflict. In one of the first countervailing duty cases under the Canada–US Free Trade Agreement (CUSFTA), a panel remanded the DOC's subsidy determination three times, finding that the DOC had not made the case that provincial stumpage fees constituted an industry-specific subsidy payment. In December 1993, Canada won the final case by a narrow margin (three to two), and the US Trade Representative took the case to the Extraordinary Challenge Committee (ECC), alleging a conflict of interest on the part of the two Canadian panellists. The challenge was struck down, and the DOC terminated the countervailing duty order in 1994. The United States threatened to keep the duties collected, but ultimately agreed to refund them. In 1996, the Softwood Lumber Agreement was signed, restricting Canadian lumber exports for five years.

The fourth and current round of the softwood battle began on May 19, 2000 when Canada launched a judicial challenge to the current trade arrangements under NAFTA. In April 2001, the DOC investigated timber lobby allegations that Canadian lumber is subsidized and dumped on the American market. Article 2.1 of the WTO's Anti-Dumping Agreement states that "a product is to be considered as being dumped, i.e. introduced into the commerce of another country at less than its normal value, if the export price of the product exported from one country to another is less than the comparable price, in the ordinary course of trade, for the like product when destined for consumption in the exporting country." The usual test to determine dumping is a comparison of the price of the product in question on the domestic market and its price in foreign markets. The WTO's subsidy regime comes into play because firms most often make up the difference between "normal value" and export price through state support. The common assumption is most often the truth—cheap exports from developed countries are almost always heavily subsidized.

The Coalition for Fair Lumber Imports alleged that Canada's stumpage fees and log export restraints constituted a subsidy of approximately 39 per cent. Along with countervailing duty investigations, the DOC conducted a nation-wide investigation to determine whether Canadian timber was being dumped on the US market. In an interesting twist, the Maritime Provinces, where timber is harvested from private lots, were also charged with dumping despite the fact that timber regulation there is virtually identical to regulation south of the border. The International Trade Commission (ITC), whose job it is to determine whether American firms have been injured by dumping, found that there had been no material injury, only a threat of injury. The DOC found that Canadian timber was subsidized at a rate of approximately 19 per cent and that timber was being dumped on the US market at unfair prices—with dumping margins ranging from 5.94 per cent to 19.24 per cent. Since 2001, Canada has concluded eleven legal challenges—four at the NAFTA Secretariat and seven at the WTO—but trade litigation has thus far failed to deliver a judicial knockout.

Softwood became an anti-dumping issue because American industry made little headway in classifying stumpage fees as subsidies, and it now had a new weapon in its arsenal—the Byrd Amendment. If a case could be made for dumping, the subsequent subsidy case would be easier to make. Ironically, there is some question as to whether the Byrd Amendment could ever have applied to Canadian timber. NAFTA Article 1902 states that each party can amend or modify its anti-dumping laws as it sees fit, but "such amendment shall apply to goods from another Party only if the amending statute specifies that it applies to goods from that Party or from the Parties to this Agreement." Canada was never specified in the Byrd Amendment, but, strangely, litigators never exploited this omission.

NAFTA Chapter 19 Binational Panel Decisions

Canada took its cause to the NAFTA Secretariat in 2002. The panel's finding of July 17, 2003 was an unmitigated win for Canada. The panel ordered the US Department of Commerce to correct its flawed determination of dumping against Canadian lumber producers (NAFTA, 2003, July 17). In a second decision that same summer, the panel decided that Canadian stumpage fees are not countervailable subsidies under US law (NAFTA, 2003, August 13). In September of 2003, Canada won a third round at NAFTA, when the panel disagreed with the International Trade Commission's finding that Canadian lumber posed a threat of injury to American lumber producers (NAFTA, 2003, September 5). Most significantly, the extraordinary challenge launched by the US Trade Representative to appeal this decision was also in Canada's favour. On August 10, 2005, the Extraordinary Challenge Committee upheld the decision of the panel that determined that there was no substantial evidence that Canadian lumber exports posed a material threat to the US lumber industry (NAFTA, 2005). Under CUSFTA and then under NAFTA, panels consistently ruled that Canada's softwood lumber industry did not pose a threat of injury to American producers.

WTO Panel Decisions

On May 19, 2000, Canada requested consultations with the United States regarding the determination that Canada's export restraint on unprocessed logs was a subsidy to other producers who use logs as a manufacturing input (WTO DSB, 2000, October 27). The United States argued that the export restraint lowered the price of logs for domestic mills. The panel's report, released on June 29, 2001, found that "an export restraint as defined in this dispute cannot constitute government-entrusted or government-directed provision of goods in the sense of subparagraph (iv) and hence does not constitute a financial contribution in the sense of Article 1.1(a) of the SCM Agreement." The first round was a substantial win for Canada.

In August of 2001, Canada again requested consultations with the United States, this time concerning the DOC's preliminary countervailing duty determination against Canadian softwood (WTO DSB, 2001–2007). The panel report released on September 27, 2002 was Canada's second win. The panel found that the DOC's preliminary countervailing duty determination was not inconsistent with Article 1.1 (a) of the SCM Agreement. This means that the DOC did not err when it classified Canadian stumpage fees as a subsidy—it is possible to make a successful legal argument that stumpage fees convey a financial contribution. However, the United States failed to determine whether a material benefit had been conferred on Canadian harvesters by current stumpage rates. It also failed to establish that a benefit was conferred to Canadian mills through Canada's stumpage program and log export restraint. Therefore, the panel decided that the DOC's countervailing duty determination was inconsistent with US obligations under the Subsidy and Countervailing Measures Agreement. At the implementation phase, the United States argued that it had implemented the panel's recommendations because the particular countervailing duties (CVDs) in question were no longer active. Canada responded that the United States had not changed the trade legislation that allowed for the original determinations. The next panel on the same issue was released in August of 2003. The panel ruled that the ITC had acted inconsistently with SCM obligations because it failed to analyse properly the material injury suffered by American timber harvesters (WTO DSB, 2002–2007). It did, however, rule upon the basic legality of challenging Canada's regulatory model. The Appellate Body (AB) upheld the panel's finding that provincial methods for granting timber rights are actionable under the SCM. The United States reported that it would comply with the AB recommendations for implementation, but it later announced that a new countervailing duty determination from the DOC was forthcoming, and it would wait to see the outcome of the newest investigation. Canada launched a compliance panel, which reconfirmed that the United States remained in violation of its treaty obligations.

The fourth case dealt with the DOC's determination that Canadian lumber was dumped on the American market. Canada argued that the DOC erred by using a "zeroing" methodology to calculate dumping duties. "Zeroing" treats price comparisons that do not show dumping as zero values in the calculation of a weighted average dumping margin.[3] This means that, when calculating the dumping margins, the DOC did not factor into calculations the Canadian timber sold at higher prices—zeroing these transactions instead of factoring them into the equation—which allowed the DOC to levy higher anti-dumping duties and penalties. The panel found that the DOC failed to comply with the requirements of the Anti-Dumping Agreement when it did not take into account all export transactions by applying the "zeroing" methodology when calculating the margin of dumping. The Appellate Body agreed.

The final case dealt with the International Trade Commission's finding that Canadian timber posed a threat to the US industry (WTO DSB, 2002–2006). In its report released March 22, 2004, the panel found that the ITC failed to comply with the requirements of Article 3.5 and 3.7 of the

Anti-Dumping Agreement and 15.5 and 15.7 of the Subsidy and Counter-vailing Measures Agreement in finding a causal link between imports and the threat of injury to the domestic softwood industry. The Appellate Body upheld the panel's decision. At the end of November 2004, the DOC revisited its method for calculating dumping duties. The methodology was revised based on a transaction-to-transaction comparison of the "normal value" of Canadian lumber on the domestic market and its price in the United States. This method was justified under Article 2.4.2 of the AD, which allows such comparisons. Canada disagreed and launched a compliance dispute. The panel reported back in April of 2006, allowing the DOC's revised dumping methodology (WTO DSAB, 2006). Similarly, the ITC amended its methodology for determining material injury, and, in the compliance phase of DS277, the panel upheld the legality of its new methods. These two cases are the only ones to undermine Canada's legal position vis-à-vis American softwood producers. Subsequently, DS264 and DS277 will likely be hinge cases around which the US industry will make a future legal foray.

Related WTO Panel Decisions

Two other cases not directly related to softwood are also central to this dispute. The first is a Canadian complaint against section 129(c)(1) of the Uruguay Round Agreements Act (an act of the US Congress). This legislation requires that authorities not consider Dispute Settlement Body rulings when making dumping determinations. The Canadian case against this act was especially difficult to make because nothing in WTO law requires that states formulate domestic law explicitly under the rubric of completed WTO agreements. If legislation is inconsistent with WTO obligations, members may raise the issue through dispute settlement. The panel ruled in July of 2002 that Canada had not made its case that section 129(c)(1) of the Uruguay Round Agreements Act was inconsistent with American obligations under the GATT, AD, and SCM agreements (WTO DSB, 2002, July 15).

The second was Canada's and Mexico's complaint about the Continued Dumping and Subsidy Offset Act of 2000 (CDSOA), commonly known as the Byrd Amendment.[4] The CDSOA changed the way that dumping duties are collected. Rather than going into the US treasury, duties were placed into separate accounts set up for each anti-dumping case. At the end of the fiscal year, they were distributed to companies directly involved in the case. Along with Australia, Brazil, Chile, the European Communities (EC), India, Indonesia, Japan, Korea, and Thailand, Canada and Mexico argued that the Continued Dumping and Subsidy Offset Act of 2000 nullified or impaired benefits accruing to the complaining parties under the GATT, SCM, and AD agreements, and the panel agreed. However, in its report, the panel also

Figure 2.1. *Anatomy of the Softwood Dispute*

NAFTA Chapter 19 Panel Decisions

USA-CDA-2002-1904-2 *Win for Canada.* The panel ordered US Department of Commerce to correct its flawed dumping determination.

USA-CDA-2002-1904-3 *Win for Canada.* The panel decided that Canadian stumpage fees are not countervailable subsidies under US law.

USA-CDA-2002-1904-7 *Win for Canada.* The panel disagreed with the United States International Trade Commission's determination that Canadian lumber posed a threat of material injury for American producers.

NAFTA Extraordinary Challenge Committee (ECC) Decision

ECC-2004-1904-01USA *Win for Canada.* The ECC upheld the decision of the panel in USA-CDA-2002-1904-7.

WTO Dispute Settlement (DS) Panel Decisions

DS194 *Win for Canada.* The panel found that an export restraint does not constitute a financial contribution in the sense determined by Article 1.1(a) of the SCM Agreement.

DS236 *Win for Canada.* The panel found that the US Department of Commerce's imposition of countervailing duties was inconsistent with American obligations under the SCM Agreement.

DS257 *Win for Canada.* The Panel found that the US Department of Commerce's imposition of countervailing duties was inconsistent with American obligations under the GATT and the SCM Agreement.

DS264 *Win for Canada.* The panel found that the US Department of Commerce failed to comply with the Anti-Dumping (AD) Agreement when it used a "zeroing" method to calculate dumping margins.

DS277 *Win for Canada.* The panel found that the US International Trade Commission failed to comply with the SCM and AD agreements when it found a causal link between imports and the threat of injury to the American softwood industry.

Related WTO Dispute Settlement (DS) Panel Decisions

DS221 *Win for the United States.* The panel ruled that Canada had not made its case that section 129(c)(1) of the Uruguay Round Agreements Act was inconsistent with American obligations under the GATT, AD, and SCM agreements.

DS234 *Win for Canada.* The panel found that the Continued Dumping and Subsidy Offset Act of 2000 (Byrd Amendment) nullified or impaired benefits to the complaining parties under the GATT, AD, and SCM agreements.

Sources: Foreign Affairs and International Trade Canada (2009), Rahman and Devadoss (2002).

noted that this sort of legislation is a new and complex issue for the WTO because it deals with the use of subsidies as trade remedies — a sensitive area where industrial policy and trade governance intersect. The Appellate Body upheld the main provisions of the panel report. In April 2005, the European Communities and Canada notified the Dispute Settlement Body that they were suspending trade concessions under the GATT on imports of certain products originating in the United States in retaliation for American non-compliance with the panel ruling.

By the end of 2005, the United States repealed the Byrd Amendment. Congress's Government Accountability Office reported that duties collected, far from being a form of support for firms contending with unfair trade practices, were in fact a highly lucrative system of payments going to only a handful of companies, three of which were related (United States Government Accountability Office, 2005). In Congress, prominent Democrats and Republicans agreed that the Byrd Amendment was, in the words of Jim Ramstad (R–MN) "the ultimate combination of protectionism, corporate welfare, and government waste" (Odessey, 2005).

On April 27, 2006, Canada and the United States agreed to a truce. The United States agreed to lift the 10 per cent countervailing duty on softwood imports and agreed to refund 80 per cent of the $5 billion in duties collected. Canada agreed to cap its market share at 34 per cent by collecting a sliding tax that rises as the price of lumber in the United States falls below $355 per thousand board feet.[5] This deal is in place for seven years, with an option to renew for two more years. There are few substantive differences between this deal and the Softwood Lumber Agreement (SLA) negotiated in 1996. The combination of export charges and volume restraints in this deal is remarkably similar to the fees charged for exceeding quantitative limits set out in the SLA. This is the third time Canada has imposed quantitative restrictions on its lumber industry.

WHEN NATIONAL REGULATORY MODELS COLLIDE

The outcome of Canada's softwood litigation has been mixed. Certainly, the sweeping wins at both the NAFTA Secretariat and the WTO reinforce the basic legality of the Canadian regulatory model. But the issue is not so clear-cut. The WTO panels allowed that stumpage fees are actionable under the SCM but disagreed with US methods for determining duties. Stumpage fees fall into the vast area in Article I of the Subsidies and Countervailing Measures Agreement, which delineates actionable, non-actionable, and prohibited subsidies. This means that stumpage fees are not illegal under WTO law, but they can be challenged by any member who can make the case that its "most favoured nation" benefits have been nullified or impaired by

Canada's framework for regulating softwood lumber harvesting. In practice, this means that, even though a deal has been reached in this round of the lumber dispute, there is nothing in US law or WTO law that would prevent future challenges to Canada's system of stumpage fees.

The putative aim of the Uruguay Round signatories was to create a flexible interface between different market economies. At least in the context of anti-dumping, this has not happened. The rise of anti-dumping actions at the WTO has created a new order of trade conflict at a time when intra-sectoral competition has increased the pressure on states to support domestic producers in a number of sectors, including agriculture, steel, textiles, wood products, and high value-added manufacturing, such as the production of automobiles and aircraft. In 2005, North America experienced a net trade deficit in sawn wood for the first time ever. Despite continuing high levels of production in North America, massive influx of lumber from the former Soviet states, now known as the Commonwealth of Independent States (CIS), is making deep inroads on this continent. The Russian Federation, Ukraine, and Belarus export approximately 70 per cent of their softwood production, totalling more than 15 million cubic metres. Much of it goes to China, but a significant amount of cheap timber is finding its way to North America.

Trade liberalization squeezes both Canadian and American timber producers. They have responded in a fashion according to the compensations built into their regulatory model—the Americans through recourse to aggressive trade remedies, the Canadians to government intervention in the form of competitively priced stumpage fees. What to the uninformed trade watcher appears to be a simple subsidy and trade remedy issue is in fact the clash of regulatory models due in large part to competitive pressure in the North American timber industry. (See Figure 2.2.)

The current governance environment offers several challenges and possibilities for small economies engaged in complex subsidy and anti-dumping disputes. A singular short-term challenge remains unaddressed—that of enforcing compliance against a larger competitor. In the WTO system, dispute settlement is most likely to result in an enforceable decision when the parties are of similar economic weight and share a dense set of trade relations. Small economies are often in the position of being unable to enforce compliance, and bilateral diplomacy is increasingly critical to brokering a deal, despite the fact that it always involves a number of trade-offs between domestic producers and foreign complainants. Therefore, the WTO's dispute settlement mechanism is likely in the future to continue to provide room for negotiated settlements in Canada's disputes with the United States.

On the face of it, this seems like a bit of a disappointing deal for Canada. The United States is not likely to simply comply with a panel ruling when it

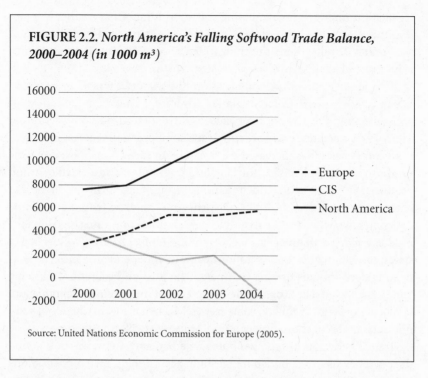

FIGURE 2.2. *North America's Falling Softwood Trade Balance, 2000–2004 (in 1000 m³)*

Source: United Nations Economic Commission for Europe (2005).

can get a better deal in negotiation. But this is the price Canada pays for living beside the world's most lucrative export market. And in many ways, this is exactly the outcome that Ottawa's experts expect. In this regard, the WTO is acting as a neutral forum for managing a political relationship. This doesn't mean that policymakers cannot hope for more; it just means that the massive economic power imbalances between Canada and the United States are not fully equalized by dispute settlement, and they never will be. How to deal with that is an ongoing challenge.

The second challenge is how to better manage the massive regulatory differences that have bedevilled the timber industry for decades. With a new deal in place until 2013, Canada must decide whether or not to defend its regulatory model in an increasingly integrated industry. Some experts argue that this defence is not possible and that long-term stability in the sector requires that Canada harmonize its policies and practices, to a greater extent, with those of the United States. However, this simple prescription misses one of the main issues.

Canada is the largest exporter of timber to the United States. Approximately 49 per cent of American timber imports come from Canada. Even if Canada were to transform its timber industries radically, it still remains the largest foreign competitor in the embattled American timber sector. Regulatory harmonization is no guarantee that Canada won't feel the protectionist pressure of the American timber lobby in the future. Nevertheless, Canadian regulators need to decide if further harmonization will reduce regulatory friction, at least in the short and medium term, or if maintaining a distinctive regulatory model is more conducive to long-term stability and growth in the sector.

CONCLUSION: THE NETWORK OF BARGAINS

The softwood lumber cases discussed above mainly dealt with relationships between governments and firms and their lobby groups. I have not dealt with other relationships that are in the background of this dispute but that, nevertheless, ought to be mentioned, the most important being the relationship between government and citizens. In the Canadian context, this relationship involves complex environmental and First Nations' issues. There is an argument to be made that stumpage fees paid for logging Crown lands are a more environmentally friendly approach to timber regulation because the costs of redeveloping timber stands can be built into the fee for each tree cut down. But, on the other hand, the issue of Crown lands is also closely related to questions regarding the use of traditional territories by Canada's First Nations, and there is another argument to be made that low stumpage rates are an incentive for rapacious timber firms to pillage the natural environment. Some environmental groups and First Nations agree with the American timber lobby that low stumpage fees are a form of industrial subsidization.

According to the *Watershed Sentinel*, an environmental newsletter published in British Columbia,

> Americans are absolutely right — in Canada, both our provincial and federal governments do subsidize logging companies in numerous ways. For starters, there were the "softwood adjustment funds" the federal government handed out to "soften" the impact of paying duties to the Americans until the dispute was settled in 2006, despite the fact most companies remained profitable while paying the added taxes. . . . But one of the biggest subsidies is also one of the most longstanding: the stumpage system itself. . . . In BC, about one in every three trees is cut at the rate of 25 cents per cubic metre. A cubic metre of tree makes a log the size of a telephone pole.[6]

Aboriginal groups and environmental activists agree that so much lumber is certainly worth more than a quarter, and, if the timber industry is not paying more, we are all losing. We are losing our natural environment, First Nations peoples are losing their traditional environment and way of life, and citizens lose jobs due to market volatility.

In the American context, the relationship between government and citizens revolves around the politicization of the softwood issue in Congress. The issue transcends partisan boundaries, coalescing around softwood producers and consumers. As long as Canada maintains governmental regulations that differ from those across the border, the American timber industry continues to advocate vociferously for trade remedy action, believing that cheap timber from Canada undercuts American profits. On the other hand, timber consumers—home builders are the most prominent—continue to advocate for freer trade in softwood lumber because they believe this will create a stable market with lower prices.

In June 2006, the American Consumers for Affordable Homes (an ad hoc umbrella group that counts in its membership a number of firms and advocacy groups, including the National Association of Home Builders and retail giant, Home Depot) posted on its website a bipartisan letter written to President Bush by a number of members of Congress, led by Jim Kolbe, a Republican from Arizona. It read, in part, as follows:

> We should help people achieve the American dream of owning their own home, and the price of lumber is a crucial component of housing costs. . . . We are concerned with a number of issues in the softwood lumber framework document. The framework document allows Canadian provinces to choose between a tax and a quota. While we would prefer neither a tax nor a quota, choosing between the two will create further uncertainty in the marketplace. The agreement also puts in place a surge mechanism that stops lumber imports from Canada when they reach a certain level. Both provisions will contribute to volatility in the marketplace, which is an enormous problem for home builders and lumber dealers and will add burdensome costs to affordable housing for those who are least able to pay.[7]

Obviously, this issue is far from clear-cut—if you would excuse the pun. We have Canadian environmental groups siding with the American timber lobby and American consumer groups siding with the Canadian government. So there is no single American or Canadian position on softwood. This case is an excellent example of the network of bargains, in which many different actors have staked out positions. The main policy issue here boils down to one of policy autonomy. Canadian harvesters and processors together are the largest competitor in the American softwood lumber market, and, as a result, any regulatory difference that may be reflected in pricing is bound to cause friction. The lesson that Canadian policymakers and politicians have taken from this round of softwood lumber dispute settlement is that litigation in this sector is a high-stakes game that boils down to hard negotiation, no matter how many panels Canada wins.

Dispute settlement did not lead to policy change. In fact, the negotiated settlement seemed to be more of the same — a pause in the dance that was all but foreseeable, given the long-term nature of this dispute. But the picture is somewhat complicated by the fact that, although the federal government is in charge of Canada's external relations, such as multilateral representation, the provinces set natural resource policy in their own jurisdictions. This is what accounts for the patchwork of stumpage fee regulations and the fact that Atlantic Canada's forestry industry looks so different from that elsewhere in the country. In British Columbia, recent changes in stumpage fees may have been related to this round of the softwood trade war, but we must bear in mind that British Columbia, which has about half of Canada's softwood inventory, is also home to an industry that has been in difficult financial straits for a number of years, and for a number of reasons. Government seems to have a strong incentive to come to the aid of an industry that is one of the prominent employers in the province's interior (although not the economic mainstay it once was), but a significant re-evaluation of the regulatory model does not seem to be on the table. The same can be said of the industries across the west, Ontario, and Quebec.

The politically charged rhetoric, strongly polarized interest groups within a densely woven network of bargains, a deeply interconnected and continental timber industry, and price differences that are caused, at least in part, by divergent ways of regulating the industry are a potent cocktail. The newest deal may have ended this round, but the trade war is far from over.

Notes

1. The revised Anti-Dumping Agreement provides a more systematic method for determining whether a product is dumped, sets criteria for determining injury, and clarifies procedures for initiating and conducting anti-dumping investigations.
2. Nobody knows what the future trajectory of anti-dumping will look like, but Blonigen and Bown (2001) suggest that the current tit-for-tat pattern of anti-dumping actions may lead to a form of "Cold War" equilibrium.
3. For an in-depth discussion of zeroing and its effects on anti-dumping determinations, see World Trade Organization, Dispute Settlement Body (2005, October 31).
4. See the World Trade Organization, Dispute Settlement Body (2001–2006). For more information, consult the World Trade Organization's website: http://www.wto. org/english/tratop_e/dispu_e/cases_e/ds234_e.htm.
5. The basic terms of the 2006 Canada–United States Agreement on Softwood Lumber are made available by the Department of Foreign Affairs and International Trade at http://www.international.gc.ca/controls-controles/softwood-bois_ oeuvre/other-autres/agreement-accord.aspx.

6. From "Forest share: How subsidies cheat First Nation communities," by Andrew MacLeod, 2007, *Watershed Sentinel*. Read the whole article at www.watershed-sentinel.ca/content/forest-share-how-subsidies-cheat-first-nation-communities.
7. Read the whole letter on the website of the American Consumers for Affordable Homes: www.acah.org/061306.htm.

CHAPTER THREE

State Trading Enterprises: The Case of the Canadian Wheat Board

Agriculture is one of Canada's leading value-added industries. Wheat prices are somewhat cyclical and have a higher variable of growth compared to prices in the total Canadian business sector. In Canada, market volatility has been managed through wheat pooling and the international sale of wheat through a single-desk marketing system. Like all agricultural exporters, Canada has a number of programs in place to deal with volatility in global markets for agricultural products. In the United States, price swings are managed by direct payments to exporters through a number of subsidy programs administered by the US Department of Agriculture's Foreign Agricultural Service. Like American farm support programs, the Canadian Wheat Board (CWB) plays an important political role in stabilizing the agricultural sector alongside its commercial function of maximizing wheat sales for farmers (Cross, 2007).

Interestingly, trade in the agriculture sector does not play the same pivotal role on the prairies that it once did. Oil and natural gas now dominate the Alberta economy. Likewise in Saskatchewan, mineral exports are worth three and a half times the value of agricultural exports. In Manitoba, manufacturing accounts for 12 per cent of the economy, and agriculture, mining, and forestry account for a combined total of 7 per cent of GDP, rather inconsequential considering the fact that wheat and ranching used to be the primary industries on the prairies. The significant proportion of eastern European surnames between Winnipeg and Calgary is attributable to the fact that Clifford Sifton, minister of the interior under Sir Wilfrid Laurier, pushed hard to recruit hardy peasant farmers from Ukraine and surrounding areas because he believed that they were best suited to take on the harsh farming challenges of the prairies. My paternal grandfather was one of those who emigrated from Russia in 1926, drawn by the promise of religious freedom and plenty of land in the Canadian west.

The Canadian Wheat Board came into existence in 1919. It was the result of farmers becoming frustrated with what they considered to be exploitation by the railways, line elevator companies, and the Winnipeg Grain Exchange. In 1912, the Canada Grain Act established the Canadian Grain Commission as the official inspector of grain. During World War I, the federal government became directly involved in grain marketing and created the Board of Grain Supervisors (BGS). In 1917, the BGS suspended trading in wheat futures on the Winnipeg Grain Exchange and took direct control of the pricing, marketing, and sale of wheat. Two years later, the BGS was replaced by the Canadian Wheat Board. Over the intervening decades, farmers have taken a direct hand in the governance of the Wheat Board, most recently in 1998, when an amendment to the Canada Grain Act created a fifteen-person board of directors, ten of which are farmer-elected directors. Far from being a monolith, the Canadian Wheat Board actually controls very few agricultural commodities — currently, it only oversees wheat and barley destined for human consumption. Significant cash crops like canola do not fall under its purview at all.

The CWB was an important player in world wheat markets during the Cold War. Following World War II, Canada became one of the world's leading suppliers of grain, sending this important staple to liberated European countries before the drought in the late 1940s limited Canadian supplies. In the 1950s and 60s, the CWB signed agreements with China and the Soviet Union to supply millions of tons of wheat. These massive communist states were concentrating on industrial development and could not meet wheat production needs internally. These long-term purchase agreements cut out grain agents and took western Canadian wheat directly to the buyer. This arrangement suited Canadian farmers who wanted to sell a lot of wheat, and it fit the needs of communist states, which required a stable supply of grain. Today, farmers have many more options for the global marketing and sale of their products. Some farmers value the CWB brand and are happy to allow this long-standing institution to market and sell their product. Others chafe under government bureaucracy, preferring greater marketing freedom to the stability of the CWB.

When the federal Conservative Party of Canada came to power with a minority government in 2006, it made dismantling the Wheat Board an important goal. There are two concerns highlighted by opponents of the CWB. First, only western Canadian farmers must sell to the Wheat Board.

Farmers in other parts of Canada have separate marketing boards, and participation is voluntary. Second, there is some evidence that the current system forces farmers and taxpayers to bear hidden costs (Carter & Loyns, 1996). In response, proponents of the CWB argue that farmers are protected to a certain degree from market volatility and that the Canadian Wheat Board brand is known globally for its high-quality product. They propose that the Wheat Board is not outdated, merely underappreciated. Meanwhile, south of the border, the main issue for American competitors is structural. They believe that the Canadian Wheat Board is structured in such a way as to ensure it will not operate in accordance with commercial considerations — that is, in the interests of free market competition.

Canada–Wheat Exports and Grain Imports was the first WTO panel report to consider the substance of Canada's marketing model for western Canadian wheat and barley. It was also the first test of the WTO's regulation of state trading enterprises (STEs) under GATT Article XVII. The first part of this chapter contains an overview of the place of state trading enterprises in international trade and examines the cases for and against this form of producer support. The second portion of the chapter examines the WTO panel and Appellate Body reports in the 2004 Canada–Wheat case. The WTO panel found that the primary discipline of GATT Article XVII:1 governing STEs was non-discrimination and that operating on the basis of "commercial considerations," as commerce was defined in the American argument, was not an independent obligation.

The final section examines the convergence of Canadian and American levels of support for agriculture. In this case, the WTO upheld the legality of Canada's state trading enterprise, suggesting that trade discipline may impact Canadian industrial policy less than other factors such as proximity to American markets and other competitive pressures that result from increased exposure to global markets. Both Canada and the United States are adjusting levels of support downwards overall, and each country responds to the pressures of intra-sectoral competition in different ways. What then is the future of the Canadian Wheat Board? Are its days numbered?

The conclusion examines the network of bargains around this case, and I suggest that the Canadian Wheat Board remains a contentious institution, not because American farmers do not like it, but because it is increasingly unpopular in western Canada, especially in Alberta, where farmers often consider it to be an impediment to, rather than a support for, agricultural development. Nevertheless, the CWB remains popular in Saskatchewan and Manitoba, and, in the immediate future, the federal government needs to consider carefully the implications of removing programs that stabilize prices for domestic producers.

TRADE FRICTION IN THE NORTH AMERICAN MARKET FOR WHEAT

There are a number of different types of state trading enterprises competing in global agriculture markets. They range from statutory marketing boards (like the CWB) to canalising agencies and foreign trade enterprises. STEs are operated by the vast majority of countries that export agricultural goods. There is a small body of literature that examines the role of STEs in global agriculture markets. Much of the literature assumes that their market power stems from special privileges from and relationships with national governments and that they compete in otherwise competitive markets. Recent studies by Abbott and Kallio (1996), Pick and Carter (1994), and Veeman, Fulton, and Larue (1999) have shown that this is a problematic assumption. Much of the world grain trade is controlled by about half a dozen multinationals, including Cargill and Louis Dreyfus. International grain traders frequently "price to market," meaning that they price their grain differently in different markets, depending on a number of factors. This handful of multinational companies has a large influence on world wheat prices. Canadian Wheat Board sales totalled approximately $2.2 billion in 2003. In comparison, Cargill sales topped $60 billion, and Louis Dreyfus posted sales worth $20 billion. Canada's single-desk marketing system is a small player in a very big industry, one that does not meet the standard definition for free market competition.

Since 1995, the United States has been especially keen to curtail the activities of agricultural state trading enterprises or ban them altogether (OECD, 2001). There is a perception on the part of the American wheat industry that state trading enterprises enjoy levels of governmental support that far outstrip the support enjoyed by American farmers. Indeed, in 1995, Canadian wheat transportation legislation was significantly changed to bring it into line with WTO law. Similarly, American farm support has been retooled over the past decade as well, although the American model of agricultural support still relies almost exclusively on cash payments to farmers. The USDA's Export Enhancement Program, which was developed under the rationale that US agricultural exporters needed government support to compete with the EC's heavily subsidized agricultural sector, has been slowly phased out, replaced by other industry-specific export subsidies such as the Dairy Export Incentive Program and the Market Access Program.

The Canadian Wheat Board was established by parliament in 1935, and it still retains its headquarters in Winnipeg, the traditional gateway to the west. It is governed by a 15-person board of directors: 10 are elected farmers, 4 are appointed by the federal minister of agriculture, and the president of the board is appointed by the prime minister. The CWB acts as a marketing agent for all western Canadian wheat and barley farmers. It pays out an interim payment for crop and a final payment, the amounts of which are set by the current year's sales volumes and prices. This pooled selling system ensures predictable cash flow for farmers through pooled prices and a government price guarantee if marketing forecasts fall below expectations. Notably, in the case of wheat and malt barley, it does not allow individual farmers to choose where, when, and to whom to market their product. In all other products, farmers are not subject to the marketing control of the Canadian Wheat Board.

High levels of farm support are as old as the trade regime itself. In fact, the most glaring compromises that the original GATT signatories made with the postwar economic order were in agriculture. The North American agricultural trade environment today is the result of diverse economic policy choices made by member governments in the process of navigating the postwar trading system. Many of these policy choices were made between 1930 and 1960, and they involved what Ruggie (1982) terms a compromise with embedded liberalism.[1] The balance developed by G7 nations during this formative period allowed them to manage the social adjustment costs of increased market openness.

Trade friction in the North American agricultural sector occurs when competitors perceive an incompatibility in approaches to regulation that gives one an unfair advantage over the other. This incompatibility can be a measurable obstacle to trade, such as legislation that violates a trade agreement, but it can also be the perception or suspicion of a market-distorting practice, such as the long-standing belief that Canadian stumpage fees constitute a form of softwood industry subsidization.

American distrust of Canadian trade policy also affected the "Canada–Wheat" case. American regulators had long harboured the suspicion that Canada's centralized marketing board for wheat and barley distorts open markets by giving the Canadian Wheat Board monopsony powers at home to buy western Canadian wheat and monopoly powers abroad to sell it on the international market (Petersmann, 1998). In the discipline of economics, monopoly refers to being the only seller in a market with many buyers. Monopsony refers to being the only buyer in a market with many sellers. In the North American context, friction between support mechanisms has been a prominent trade irritant. Yet the wheat case is not a debate over economic outcomes per se. Rather, it is a continuation of the older twentieth century debate over the proper role for government in the economy.

Today, GATT regulation of trade in agriculture is concerned chiefly with quantitative restrictions and export subsidies.[2] Article XI bans quantitative restrictions on imports, with some significant exceptions—relevant ones include exceptions to export restrictions, for example, in order to address critical food shortages, as well as restrictions for the application of standards and regulation. Export subsidies are also prohibited except in the case of primary products, which are defined as any product of farm, forest, or fishery at an early stage of processing. And, in the case of primary products, export subsidies cannot be used to increase a nation's share of international trade. Domestic subsidies and domestic support measures also fall under the GATT's purview, but they are much more difficult to police. GATT Article XVII deals with the regulation of state trading enterprises. The substantive obligations of members under the rules governing state trading are non-discrimination (most favoured nation treatment), no quantitative restrictions, preservation of the value of tariff concessions (no domestic price manipulation), and transparency. In defining non-discriminatory treatment, strict most favoured nation treatment is not necessarily required. This allows a state trading enterprise to charge different prices for its products in different markets, provided that this is done for commercial reasons, that is, to meet supply and demand conditions in export markets.

State trading enterprises serve a number of purposes — income support, price stabilization, protection of public health, continuity of domestic food supply — and they can be a government revenue stream.[3] Trebilcock and Howse (2005) add that STEs are also linked to arguments having to do with self-sufficiency, national security, and the preservation of the environment and the rural way of life. Income redistribution is often the primary reason for the use of STEs. In addition to exploiting national market power by aggregating the supplies of many farmers, STEs can distribute income towards or away from farmers. In the Canadian case, the CWB acted to distribute income towards farmers. But in developing countries, governments frequently use STEs to transfer resources away from farmers (who are often the largest landowners) and toward consumers of food (Hoekman & Trachtman, 2007, p. 8).

The GATT considers STEs to be legitimate participants in trade but also recognizes that they have the potential to distort trade if they make decisions based on government instruction rather than market principles.[4] It is difficult to quantify the anticompetitive effects of export STEs because they do not usually directly subsidize exports. However, we may assume that the state trading enterprise is in place in lieu of a subsidy, and so there remains a suspicion that its behaviour will not necessarily conform to that of other private actors. Further, there is always a suspicion that ties to national governments provide unfair advantages vis-à-vis private competitors in terms of securing financing or gaining access to sensitive information about economic policy.[5]

A main concern for American wheat producers was that the Canadian

Wheat Board was using market power and discriminatory pricing behaviour as a de facto subsidization mechanism for western Canadian wheat producers by discriminating between foreign and domestic wheat behind the border. There was a concern that implicit subsidization was occurring in the economic sense, if not in the legal sense. The United States sought a finding of broad discipline on the competitive behaviour of STEs, and a case based on such a sweeping indictment had a certain amount of traction because the CWB does not necessarily maximize export profits, as a private economic actor does. Rather, it uses its market power to get the best prices for its different products in many different national markets.[6]

CANADA — MEASURES RELATING TO EXPORTS OF WHEAT AND TREATMENT OF IMPORTED GRAIN

Over the past two decades, the American wheat industry has brought more than a dozen challenges against Canada's centralized system for buying and selling wheat. (See Figure 3.1.) Beginning in the early 1990s, the US International Trade Commission (ITC) investigated charges of Canadian wheat being dumped on the American market. In 1993, US regulators took a case to the new dispute settlement process that had been agreed to in the Canada–United States Free Trade Agreement, and Canada won. Throughout the 1990s, five more challenges were launched by the ITC, the Department of Commerce (DOC), and the Government Accountability Office (GAO). Canadian wheat exports to the United States were briefly capped in 1994 and 1995. Between 2003 and 2005, duties were twice imposed on Canadian wheat by the Department of Commerce. In both cases, the finding of material injury was appealed at the NAFTA Secretariat and subsequently reversed. And then came the most serious charge—a full-court press at the WTO to find the Canadian Wheat Board and a number of other support mechanisms in contravention of both Canada's most favoured nation obligations (GATT Article III) and GATT Article XVII:1, which defines the limits of state trading.

The ensuing "Canada–Wheat" dispute concerned two aspects of Canada's regulatory apparatus for the transport and sale of wheat. These form significant portions of what Furtan (2005) has termed Canada's "national policy" concerning wheat from the prairies. The first part of the American challenge concerned Canada's export regime for wheat, the Canadian Wheat Board. It included the legal framework of the CWB, its special rights and privileges granted by the federal government and its actions with respect to wheat purchasing at home and sales abroad of Canadian wheat. The second part concerned requirements for the treatment of grain imported into Canada, which are contained in the Canada Grain Act (CGA), the Canada Grain

Figure 3.1. *US Trade Challenges to Canadian Wheat Exports, 1990–2006*

Investigation	Date	Final Determination
US ITC investigation (under section 332 of the Tariff Act of 1930)	Jun-90	Canadian wheat sold in the United States at or above market prices—no evidence of dumping
US GAO review of the CWB/AWB	Jun-92	No evidence of unfair trade practices
Canada–United States Free Trade Agreement	Feb-93	Panel ruling in favour of Canada
US ITC investigation (under section 22 of the Agricultural Adjustment Act of 1930)	Jul-94	Negotiated cap on exports to the United States for 1994–1995
Joint Commission on Grains	Oct-95	Recommendations to improve trade in both directions
US GAO (ability of STEs to distort trade)	Jun-96	No evidence that the CWB violates any existing agreements
US GAO (Canadian wheat issues)	Nov-98	No solid conclusions
US DOC (countervailing duty on live cattle from Canada)	Oct-99	No evidence that the CWB provides a subsidy to cattle producers
US ITC investigation (under section 332 of the Tariff Act of 1930)	Nov-01	Canadian wheat sold at or above US prices in all but one of 60 months examined
US Trade Representative investigation (under section 301 of the Trade Act of 1934)	Feb-02	No justification for imposing entry barriers to Canadian wheat
US DOC / US ITC & NAFTA on appeal	Aug-03 to Jun-05	Duties imposed on Canadian wheat by US DOC; lifted in 2006 after successful NAFTA appeal

US DOC / US ITC / US CIT	Aug-03 to Jul-04	Duties imposed on Canadian wheat by US DOC; duties revoked by US ITC; appeal dismissed by US Court of International Trade
US DOC / US ITC / US CIT & NAFTA on appeal	Aug-03 to Jun-05	Duties imposed on Canadian wheat by US DOC; US ITC split on injury, so decision defaults to petitioner; lifted in 2006 after successful NAFTA appeal
WTO panel and appeal (DS276 Canada–Measures relating to exports of wheat and treatment of imported grain)	Aug-04	US argument that the CWB violates GATT Article XVII dismissed at panel and appeal. Finding that three other Canadian measures violate GATT Article III

Source: Canadian Wheat Board (2008).

Regulations, and the Canada Transportation Act. Section 57c of the Canada Grain Act governs the receipt of foreign grain into Canadian elevators. Section 56(1) of the Canada Grain Regulations disallowed the mixing of certain types of foreign and domestic grain in Canadian elevators. Section 150 of the Canada Transportation Act imposed a cap on revenues earned by certain railways for the transportation of western Canadian grain. Finally, section 87 of the CGA allows producers to apply for a railway car to transport their wheat to a grain elevator or a consignee.

Together, these measures add up to a policy that protects Canadian wheat producers from the vagaries of the international market and from significantly increased transportation costs caused by seasonal demand for railway transportation. The American case claimed that these were also trade distorting measures that gave Canadian wheat producers an unlawful set of trading advantages, in terms of both sale on the international market and the treatment of grain at home, vis-à-vis imported wheat.

The Panel Report
The American claim under GATT Article XVII:1 was a challenge to the entire CWB export regime. The American suit alleged that the illegality of the CWB export regime proceeded from a combination of three elements: the CWB's legal structure and mandate, its privileges and the incentives that flowed

from those privileges, and the lack of supervision by the Canadian government (para. 6.18–21, 6.24–25). In particular, the United States made three claims. First, the CWB export regime is not consistent with GATT Article XVII:1. Second, Canadian grain segregation requirements in section 56 of the Canada Grain Regulations and section 57 of the Canada Grain Act are inconsistent with GATT Article III:4 (national treatment) and the Trade-Related Investment Measures (TRIMs) Article 2 (investment). Third, the rail revenue cap and the producer railway car program were also inconsistent with the national treatment principle enshrined in GATT Article III and TRIMS Article 2.[7]

The United States claimed that the CWB export regime "necessarily results" in nonconforming sales because privileges enjoyed by the CWB give it more flexibility than would be enjoyed by a commercial actor. These privileges include pricing flexibility that allows the CWB to offer "non-commercial" sales terms. Furthermore, the CWB's mandate and legal structure create an incentive for it to maximize sales rather than profits, meaning that it can discriminate between markets, selling lower in some markets, for example. Finally, the United States argued that the Government of Canada does not ensure that the CWB conforms to Article XVII:1 (a) and (b) and that, in the absence of government safeguards, the CWB's legal structure and mandate result in nonconforming sales of wheat.

The panel decided that these assertions must be taken together in order to demonstrate nonconforming sales, so the United States had to establish the veracity of all four assertions. It proceeded to examine the first part of the American challenge — that the CWB's legal structure gives it an incentive to make sales that do not conform to its obligations under GATT Article XVII:1. The panel disagreed, noting that the majority of directors that serve on the CWB are elected by Canadian wheat and barley producers. These directors ensure returns for producers by maximizing sales. It also noted that the Canadian Wheat Board Act requires directors and officers to "act honestly and in good faith with a view to the best interests of the [CWB]" (para. 6.123–134). The CWB's legal structure does not give it an incentive to make wheat sales on a basis other than commercial considerations.

The panel also rejected the US assertion that the CWB's mandate to strive for a "reasonable price" meant that the CWB did not strive for a profit-maximizing price. The panel decided that, although the CWB was not striving to make a profit for itself, it was attempting to maximize the returns for its producers. Further, according to the panel, GATT Article XVII:1 does not suggest that STEs only meet the "commercial considerations" requirement if operations are structured to maximize profit. They can also be structured to meet other goals that benefit its producers, such as the maximization of returns. The panel concluded that "(a) the United States has not established that the CWB Export Regime necessarily results in non-conforming CWB export sales; and, as a consequence (b) the United States has not established that Canada has breached its obligations under Article XVII:1 of the GATT 1994" (para. 6.151).

The panel examined the other charges brought against Canada's wheat export regime. Section 57(c) of the Canada Grain Act does not allow elevators to receive foreign grain except when authorized by regulation or the Canadian Grain Commission. It found that the section is inconsistent with GATT Article III:4 because imported grain is treated less favourably than domestic grain, as an additional regulatory burden must be met by foreign grain before it can enter Canada's grain-handling system.

Turning next to an examination of the consistency of section 57(c) of the Canada Grain Act (receipt of foreign grain) with GATT Article XX (d), Canada's defence of its differential treatment of foreign grain in its domestic grain-handling system invoked the general exceptions clause of GATT. Canada argued that section 57(c) was necessary to ensure compliance with wheat grading requirements and to make sure that foreign wheat is not misrepresented as domestic wheat in Canada and elsewhere. The panel found that Canada could put policies into place that would do the same things it was intending to do without placing an extra regulatory burden on foreign wheat; therefore section 57(c) of the Canada Grain Act was not justified under GATT Article XX(d). Likewise, section 56(1) of the Canada Grain Regulations allows the mixing of any grade of grain coming into or going out of an elevator as long as neither is western grain or foreign grain. The United States argued that this is a discrimination in contravention of GATT Article III:4 because it is based on place of origin, not on whether the products are "like products." The panel also found that this section was inconsistent with GATT. Canada made the same GATT Article XX(d) defence as it had in the matter of the receipt of foreign grain, and the panel struck down this defence for the same reasons.

In the examination of the consistency of sections 150(1) and 150(2) of the Canada Transportation Act (rail revenue cap) with GATT Article III:4, the United States argued that "the effect of these provisions taken together is that domestic grain is favoured over like imported grain" in that there is an incentive for railways to hold prices down for western Canadian grain, but no incentive exists for the transportation of foreign grain (para. 6.328). Canada responded that "the revenue cap has never been met and is unlikely to be met in the future"; therefore no adverse trade effects have ever been felt by foreign grain (para. 6.357–358). The panel emphasized that it is not necessary to demonstrate adverse trade effects because GATT Article III protects the conditions of competition, and it struck down the rail revenue cap.

The panel ruled in Canada's favour in the final two allegations brought by the United States. Section 87 of the Canada Grain Act allows producers of grain who meet certain conditions to apply for a railway car to take their grain to an elevator. The United States argued that this mechanism was discriminatory because it allowed only domestic producers to access the railway car program. The panel disagreed, ruling that there was nothing in the statute that limited access to railway cars to domestic producers. Finally, the United States claimed that section 87 of the Canada Grain Act is inconsistent with TRIMs Article 2 because it "requires shippers to use domestic Canadian grain in order to obtain an advantage." Recalling its finding above, the panel ruled that because the United States had not established that section 87 excluded foreign producers, it was not necessarily inconsistent with TRIMs Article 2.1.

The Appellate Body Report

The dispute settlement panel in the wheat case took the view that the term "commercial" simply refers to economic action that is actually taking place in the marketplace. The United States had sought to define the term "commercial" as referring to an undistorted free market. The panel decided that the term, although it referred to business interaction within the market, did not preclude goals other than profit (Hoekman & Trachtman, 2007, p. 30).[8] This interpretation of GATT Article XVII:1 preserved a significant realm of autonomy and scope of action for STEs. This is significant in the Canadian context because the panel ruled that the CWB's approach to grain exports that maximizes sales for farmers rather than profits from individual transactions is a perfectly legitimate way for an STE to conduct business in the global marketplace.

The Appellate Body adopted an interpretation of GATT Article XVII:1 that limits its disciplines to non-discrimination. STE action need not conform to free-market expectations; it must only be non-discriminatory. It declined to find a requirement that STEs act like private actors and, in this way, preserved the ability of states to use STEs to achieve broader public policy goals (Hoekman & Trachtman, 2007, p. 3). The finding suggests that certain government policies and agencies, including STEs, "may be appropriate responses to the exercise of market power by large multinational corporations in particular fields" (Hoekman & Trachtman, 2007, p. 18). The fact that this approach has the dual outcome of preserving significant global

Figure 3.2. *Anatomy of the Wheat Dispute*

Examination of the legality of Canada's export regime for wheat

- CWB's legal structure does not give it an incentive to make wheat sales on a basis other than commercial considerations. The panel also rejected the US assertion that the CWB's mandate to strive for a "reasonable price" meant that the CWB did not strive for a profit-maximizing price. The panel decided that, although the CWB was not striving to make a profit for itself, it was attempting to maximize the returns for its producers. Further, it determined that GATT Article XVII:1 does not suggest that STEs meet the "commercial considerations" requirement if operations are structured only to maximize profit. They can also be structured to meet other goals that benefit its producers, such as the maximization of returns.

Examination of the consistency of section 57(c) of the Canada Grain Act (receipt of foreign grain) with GATT Article III

- The panel found that the section was inconsistent because imported grain was treated less favourably than domestic grain.

Examination of the consistency of section 57(c) of the Canada Grain Act (receipt of foreign grain) with GATT Article XX (d)

- The panel found that Canada could put policies into place that would do the same things it was intending to do without placing an extra regulatory burden on foreign wheat and therefore section 57(c) of the Canada Grain Act was not justified under GATT Article XX(d).

Examination of the consistency of section 56(1) of the Canada Grain Regulations (mixing authorization) with GATT Article III:4

- The panel found that the section was inconsistent with GATT.

Examination of the consistency of section 56(1) of the Canada Grain Regulations (mixing authorization) with GATT Article XX(d)

- The panel struck down the rail revenue cap.

Examination of the consistency of section 87 of the Canada Grain Act (producer railway cars) with GATT Article III:4

- The panel ruled that there was nothing in the statute that limited access to railway cars to domestic producers and therefore section 87 of the CGA was consistent with GATT.

Examination of the consistency of section 87 of the Canada Grain Act (producer railway cars) with TRIMs Article 2

- The panel ruled that, because the United States had not established that section 87 excluded foreign producers, it was not necessarily inconsistent with TRIMs Article 2.1.

market share for Canadian farmers while simultaneously sheltering producers from unstable international wheat prices is of no legal consequence. It is smart public policy, not anticompetitive behaviour.

THE FUTURE OF THE CANADIAN WHEAT BOARD

The American response to competitive pressure on the agricultural front has been a multi-pronged attack on the Canadian Wheat Board that includes domestic trade challenges, WTO dispute settlement, and continued pressure on Canadian agricultural industries at the WTO. In the larger scheme of things, this panel decision may be significant for the global regulation of export STEs, but, in the North American context, the ruling will likely have little impact on Canada–US trade relations in the agricultural sector. Canada is the largest trade competitor with the United States in important staples sectors, from softwood to beef cattle to hard red spring wheat. In this case in particular, that the CWB is a strategic competitor may be as much the issue as how it organizes its commercial undertakings.

WTO litigation has become a part of international competition strategies — especially in trade relationships that exhibit heterogeneous models for domestic commercial regulation and divergent policy goals for the outcome of international competition. National support for agricultural producers has been steadily declining over the past 20 years, and farmers in both countries have had to manage that structural adjustment process. Farmers in Canada and the United States respond to the pressures of increased intra-sectoral competition in ways that are compatible with historical trends in agricultural support in their respective national jurisdictions. In the United States, that means action in response to interest group pressure for greater export subsidies and trade litigation.

The OECD's producer support estimates provide an indicator of the annual value of "gross transfers from consumers and taxpayers to support agricultural producers, measured at farm gate level." The Producer Support Estimate (PSE) measures transfers to farmers from policies designed to maintain domestic prices, provide payments to farmers, and support farmers through lower production input costs (OECD, 2002, p. 128). In sheer dollar amounts, the United States outspends Canada in supporting agricultural producers according to the OECD. Producer support estimates measure a significant amount of both direct and indirect state support. When using the most commonly accepted measure of producer support, Canada's policies seem to offer less support to producers and therefore are less trade distorting. Figure 3.3 shows the producer support estimates for the nations with the highest farm subsidies.

Figure 3.3. *The Apparent Gap between American and Canadian Support for Agricultural Producers: OECD Producer Support Estimates, 1986–2006 (in millions USD)*

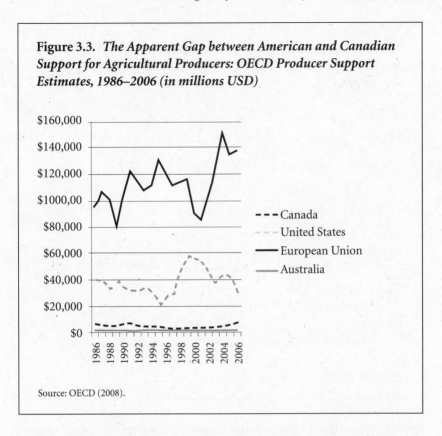

Source: OECD (2008).

The comparison of Canadian and American producer support obscures a more complex story. When producer *and* consumer support are factored together, Canada and the United States exhibit a steady trend towards lower levels of agricultural support as a percentage of GDP. (See Figure 3.4.) Total support estimates measure the "value of all gross transfers from taxpayers and consumers arising from policy measures which support agriculture" (OECD, 2002, p. 128). Total support for agriculture has declined significantly over the past 20 years. Farmers in both countries are dealing with long-term structural adjustment in their agriculture sectors. Notably, the gap between Canadian and American levels of support has narrowed considerably since the mid 1980s, when Canada offered considerably more support to farmers than did the United States.

In Canada, the overall decline in support for the agricultural sector has been the result of budgetary cutbacks, mainly on the part of the federal government. Skogstad (2008) has noted that Ottawa eliminated export grain subsidies in the 1995 federal budget, exceeding the 36 per cent target set by

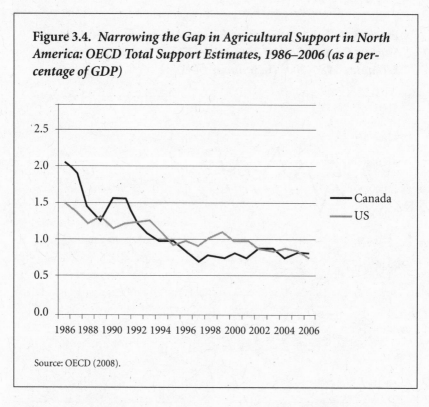

Figure 3.4. *Narrowing the Gap in Agricultural Support in North America: OECD Total Support Estimates, 1986–2006 (as a percentage of GDP)*

Source: OECD (2008).

the WTO. Even in sensitive supply-managed sectors, the Canadian government has met and sometimes exceeded WTO targets. Given Canada's historical industrial development trajectory, which has moved from centralized public ownership to decentralization over the past two decades, the CWB may be something of an anachronism, although Skogstad (2008) has also shown that patterns of continuity and change in Canadian agriculture owe moreto authoritative domestic political actors than to the dynamics of internationalization.

CONCLUSION: THE NETWORK OF BARGAINS
The ambiguity of GATT Article XVII places state trading enterprises in a difficult position vis-à-vis charges of unfair competition. After World War II, the GATT's framers were reluctant to disallow the single most important tool for social protection. In the decades immediately following the war, STEs accounted for approximately 25 per cent of world trade, with about 90 per cent of the world's wheat exports coming under the influence of state traders (Annand, 2000). STEs are perhaps the most prominent symbol of agricultural protectionism, even as they have proven to be one of the most

prudent ways to manage the social costs of trade liberalization. Analysis of the United States–Canada wheat dispute shows the reasoning by which the WTO panel was unwilling to agree with an expanded interpretation of non-discrimination — as operating under a single intellectual model of open markets. The CWB was affirmed as a non-discriminatory mode of wheat export, even as a number of explicitly protectionist measures were disallowed by the WTO.

In this case, the network of bargains included the US and Canadian governments and farmers, who participate both as economic actors as well as citizens. Indirectly, the case also involved the interests of major agricultural corporations, which control most of the world's grain trade and stand to benefit from the end of the Canadian Wheat Board because it is safe to assume that farms are not going to market their own wheat. Provincial governments, namely Alberta, also played a role in this bargaining network by stating a preference in terms of the future of the CWB. The relationship between government and farmers is perhaps the most pertinent in this case because the CWB was designed with their support in mind, and it is farmers who will be directly affected by any changes in the current legislation.

Once again, there is no particular Canadian position on the question of the Wheat Board's future. Farmers appear to be split on the issue. On the American side, there is more unanimity. American farmers and the American government consider the Wheat Board to be an unfair use of state resources to support farmers who are fully capable of competing on a global level. They may have a point. In some ways, the Canadian Wheat Board seems to be a holdover from a different time, when Canadian businesses were not big enough or sturdy enough to hold their ground in the competitive global marketplace. However, policy decisions made in this area must consider all the relative merits and demerits of this model for the export and sale of wheat. The Canadian model is weighted in favour of price security and predictability. The American alternative is weighted in favour of freer competition amongst producers and a greater role for corporate agribusiness in the marketing and sale of hard red spring wheat. The Canadian model is weighted in favour of selling more wheat rather than selling wheat for the highest possible price. The American model is predicated upon corporate growth, which, in turn, requires that corporations are profitable. This orientation toward growth and profitability frequently means that they must sell their product for the highest possible price.

The CWB is deeply rooted in Canada's historical trajectory of industrial development. Moving to a decentralized model for the marketing of western Canadian wheat will not necessarily lessen trade friction as long as western Canadian farmers are in direct competition with their American counterparts. However, it will devolve marketing and pricing authority for wheat and barley downwards to the level of producer. In theory, this is a vote of confidence for Canada's western wheat producers. In practice, the results are likely to be more nuanced. If the Canadian Wheat Board is dismantled, large grain corporations will likely step into the void, and it is unclear whether farmers will necessarily receive a better deal than they have now, although the final choice of marketing partner will be theirs alone.

Notes

1. Embedded liberalism, as a theoretical tool to analyse different national regulatory approaches to postwar integration, has lost some of its currency. Keohane (1984) successfully argued that America's move away from the gold standard ended American economic hegemony and marked the end of postwar embedded liberalism. Markets are now global, and the distinction between national and international business transactions has lost some of its significance. Nevertheless, trade friction still arises from different public policy strategies that are rooted in historical compromises with embedded liberalism.

2. Prior to the WTO Agreement, the GATT placed fewer restrictions on agriculture than it did on other sectors. Special treatment in agriculture was largely a reflection of the influence of the United States after World War II. As a result, import quotas and export subsidies became an essential part of the American supply management framework for agricultural products.

3. As of October 2007, 71 out of 151 members had notified the WTO that they are now operating or have in the past seven years operated a state trading enterprise. The number of members operating STEs is likely to be much higher given the notoriously low reporting rate. The annual reports of the WTO's Working Party on State Trading Enterprises are available through the WTO website at http://www.wto.org/english/tratop_e/statra_e/statra_e.htm.

4. OECD research has shown that economists need to differentiate between the monopoly aspect of an STE and its objective function. The assumption is frequently made that STEs will act like private firms in a monopoly position. However, "the public nature of the state trading enterprise distinguishes it from a private firm . . . although a state trading enterprise may hold a monopoly position, it may not behave in a traditional textbook manner" (OECD 2001, p. 54).

5. Hoekman & Trachtman (2007, p. 4) give five ways that STEs can be used to circumvent WTO commitments. First, they can circumvent the "most favoured nation" (MFN) principle enshrined in GATT Article I by discriminating among trade partners regarding purchases and sales. Second, they can circumvent the "national treatment" principle of GATT Article III by discriminating between domestic and imported goods. (Canada lost on this point in its treatment of for-

eign wheat at Canadian elevators.) Third, if they have import privileges, they can restrict quantities of imports against GATT Article XI. Fourth, they might exercise import rights to sell imported goods at markups that operate like tariffs. Finally, STEs may use their purchases and sales to subsidize sellers and buyers.

6. The CWB exploits quality differences in wheat grades in order to leverage higher prices across many national markets. However, its ultimate goal is to sell as much wheat as possible rather than to sell wheat at the highest possible price. Nevertheless, Canadian wheat commands high prices that are a reflection of the high quality of the Canadian product.

7. Before examining this claim, the panel addressed disagreement over the meaning of the terms of GATT Article XVII:1 (a) and 1 (b):

> 1.(a) Each contracting party undertakes that if it establishes or maintains a State enterprise, wherever located, or grants to any enterprise, formally or in effect, exclusive or special privileges, such enterprise shall, in its purchases or sales involving either imports or exports, act in a manner consistent with the general principles of non-discriminatory treatment prescribed in this Agreement for governmental measures affecting imports or exports by private traders.
>
> (b) The provisions of subparagraph (a) of this paragraph shall be understood to require that such enterprises shall, having due regard to the other provisions of this Agreement, make any such purchases or sales solely in accordance with commercial considerations, including price, quality, availability, marketability, transportation and other conditions of purchase or sale, and shall afford the enterprises of the other contracting parties adequate opportunity, in accordance with customary business practice, to compete for participation in such purchases or sales (GATT 1947).

The panel noted that Canada and the United States disagreed over whether the provisions of paragraphs 1(a) and 1(b) form an obligation on the part of members to ensure that their STEs comply with certain standards or whether, as Canada argued, the provisions only require that STEs act in such a way that a member is responsible for their actions under international law, and, if a complaining party is unable to demonstrate that the STE in question is not meeting its legal obligation, then "that Member must be assumed to have honoured its undertaking" (WTO, 2004, para. 6.34–36, 6.40).

The panel examined three interpretive issues surrounding GATT XVII:1(b) — the most important being the interpretation of the first clause of subparagraph (b), which states that "such enterprises shall, having due regard to the other provisions of this Agreement, make any such purchases or sales solely in accordance with *commercial considerations*" (emphasis added). The panel did not accept the US argument that STEs must act like "commercial actors" who "maximize profit, do not enjoy government-conferred privileges, and are disciplined by market forces." In the panel's opinion, the clause simply meant that STEs must make decisions based upon commercial rather than political considerations. STEs "should seek to purchase or sell on terms that are economically advantageous for themselves, and/or their owners, members, beneficiaries, etc." (WTO, 2004, para. 6.84–88). In short, the panel determined that, although a state trading enterprise may be granted rights and privileges that have a political goal, such as support for farmers, it must operate based on commercial considerations. For example, an STE would not be acting on commercial considerations if it bought or sold on the basis of the nationality of the supplier or buyer or because of the national interest of its member government.

8. The Appellate Body report clarified the relationship between subparagraphs (a) and (b) of GATT Article XVII:1. Subparagraph (a) "sets out an obligation of non-discrimination" and subparagraph (b) "clarifies the scope of that obligation." It disagreed with the US interpretation that subparagraph (b) "establishes separate requirements that are independent of subparagraph (a)" (WTO, 2004, para. 100). The significance of this clarification is that it more fully defined the scope of GATT Article XVII:1. The American definition of "commercial" in subparagraph (b) would have established a separate obligation for WTO members and their STEs and would have narrowed the proper scope of STE activity significantly. Any STE that could not prove that its actions were only in the service of profit maximization and undistorted market competition would have been in contravention of GATT. The Appellate Body's definition of the relationship between subparagraphs (a) and (b) is narrower. It does not allow for the expansion of obligations under subparagraph (b) but rather argues that the text provides illustrative examples of discrimination that is prohibited in (a).

CHAPTER FOUR

Export Subsidies:
The Case of Bombardier
Regional Jets

The aerospace trade conflict between Canada and Brazil has been evaluated in turn as a regulatory victory for the WTO and as an intractable dispute that threatens future trade relations in the western hemisphere (Magnus, 2004). As one of the largest subsidy cases adjudicated by the WTO, this dispute provides a revealing study of the politics of trade in strategic high-tech sectors and of the impact of dispute settlement on Canadian industrial policy in the aerospace sector.

The international aerospace industry is dominated by a small number of well-established firms producing directly competing products. They operate in a high-stakes business environment, and one of their primary competition strategies involves the use of WTO dispute settlement to obstruct competitors' financing in order to capture a larger market for next-generation aircraft. In Canada's airplane trade war with Brazil, both litigants used dispute settlement to try to gain a strategic advantage by forcing competitors to restructure their financing for aircraft sales. A similar dynamic is at play in the ongoing Boeing–Airbus disputes in which both the United States and the European Union are trying to disrupt state aid for the development of competitor's new product lines. Behind this game is the knowledge that gaining competitive advantage in the civil aircraft industry requires a partnership with the public sector because government is one of the few partners willing to bankroll high-risk, multibillion-dollar projects in which returns are not realized for a decade or more.

The Agreement on Subsidies and Countervailing Measures (SCM) prohibits export subsidies, but state support (especially in the form of payments based on export performance) is often in the economic interest of members because it is the most direct way to develop high value-added manufacturing capacity. Further, for a small, open economy such as Canada's, export subsidies are an important tool for maintaining and strengthening high-tech industry. A nation's ability to prosper and grow in an era of free trade is often referred to as its economic competitiveness. Laura D'Andrea Tyson, the former chair of President Clinton's Council of Economic Advisors, defines a nation's competitiveness as the "ability to produce goods and services that meet the test of international markets, while our citizens enjoy a standard of living that is both rising and sustainable" (Tyson, 1992, p. 1). Many other public goals are contingent upon successful international competition in high-tech sectors; some of these goals are employment and regional development, technological development, national security, and even greater national prestige.[1]

This chapter probes the use of dispute settlement in an industry in which countries "pay to play," in other words, an industry that by its very nature requires a public sector investment partner. In the United States and the European Union, for example, the aerospace industry is an integral part of the defence industry and receives generous support from government for the development of military hardware. Military technology filters down into civilian applications. Canada has very little in terms of a home-grown aerospace defence industry, although recent defence contracts with foreign producers have specific clauses that subcontract work to Canadian firms.

Every country supports its industry to a greater or lesser extent for two reasons. First, trade liberalization has not lived up to its promises of high growth and full employment. Weisbrot, Barker, and Rosnick (2001) show that between 1960 and 2000, economic growth has slowed across the globe. For the poorest countries, average annual GDP growth per capita fell from a healthy annual rate of 1.9 per cent between 1960 and 1980 to a rate of just 0.5 per cent between 1980 and 2000 (all figures in constant 2000 US dollars). The growth of middle-income countries slowed as well, from approximately 3.6 per cent to less than 1 per cent over the same periods. For the world's wealthiest nations, the slowdown in GDP growth was less severe, but significant nevertheless.

Second, the rise in competitive pressure caused by globalization requires that countries restructure domestic markets, rework the public/private mix in the provision of goods, and even back national champions if domestic firms are not strong enough to compete successfully by themselves. Especially in information and high-tech sectors, government has been actively involved in the creation of competition strategies. Government support in the form of export financing has been crucial to the success of Bombardier,

Canada's premier aircraft producer. Airplanes are big-ticket ($20–$200 million dollars per plane), low-volume products with long service lives. Airlines buy in bulk, often purchasing a dozen planes or more, with options to buy more. International competition for these billion-dollar deals is fierce, and state support has been instrumental in securing Canada's share of this global industry, just as it has for Brazil, Japan, the United States, and the European Union.

The first part of this chapter examines the role of subsidies in industrial policy and surveys the economic argument for subsidizing high-tech industries as part of a national industrial strategy. The second section provides a study of dispute settlement in this area. The WTO has had little impact on the way that Canada structures its system of high-tech subsidies. In this case, as in the softwood case, litigation led to bilateral negotiations. The final section explores the policy implications of dispute settlement in the aerospace sector. Even though litigation did not resolve the dispute, it did have an impact on the way that Canada structures its state support and on the way in which it responds to the subsidy programs of national competitors. WTO litigation has become a weapon in the arsenal of member countries pursuing industrial strategies in the high-tech sector.

The conclusion once again places this dispute in the context of its network of bargains. Dispute settlement adds a level of complexity to international competition. In this set of cases, the relationship between governments and firms was the most significant. In the previous cases I have discussed, it is not always immediately clear which business interests are the strongest driving force behind the dispute. Often, corporate players cloak themselves in the garb of citizen activists, forming groups such as the Coalition for Fair Lumber Imports. But, in this case, Canada and Brazil were backing national champions. As champions, Bombardier and Embraer provide thousands of high-paying jobs and produce high-tech products that convey status upon their nation's manufacturing sectors. Canada is known around the world for Bombardier trains, planes, and snowmobiles. Likewise, Embraer aircraft are the pride of Brazil.

This set of cases is widely considered to be a regulatory victory because it clarified the WTO's position on the use of export subsidies by developing countries. Nevertheless, the WTO is contending with the double standard of its members when it comes to export subsidies. As a result, the current configuration of rules is likely to become a lightning rod for disputes involving developed countries protecting strategic industries and developing countries attempting to build industrial capacity in high value-added areas such as aerospace, auto assembly, and electronics.

SUBSIDIES, TRADE, AND ECONOMIC GROWTH

Research, development, and production subsidies are essential tools in Canada's strategy for high-tech industries because technology-intensive manufacturing often requires an economic commitment above and beyond what most private capital is able to provide. Especially in small economies, the choice is often between government intervention and foreign ownership, a stark choice that Canada has faced many times in the past. This is uncontroversial; most economists agree that state support is sometimes required for economic development. There is also consensus, however, that export subsidies are of a different order than other forms of industrial support and should be prohibited (De Meza, 1989).

The rationale for greater subsidies discipline is based upon evidence that export subsidies harm the economies of other countries and are therefore anticompetitive (Slaughter, 2003). Any subsidies with a direct impact on trade are prohibited. In the past, international agreements such as the General Agreement on Tariffs and Trade (GATT) failed to define subsidy action comprehensively (Lee, 2002). In 1994, negotiators agreed for the first time and defined the term "subsidy" in the first article of the Agreement on Subsidies and Countervailing Measures (SCM). Article I of the SCM declares, "a subsidy shall be deemed to exist if . . . there is a financial contribution [and] . . . a benefit is conferred."[2] Government action can be classed as a subsidy if it imposes a direct cost on the public sector; if government does not receive equivalent compensation for the incentive given; if government intervenes in order to achieve a certain market outcome, such as a price change; or if the action targets a specific set of market actors (Lehner, Meiklejohn, & Reichenbach, 1991).

The SCM Agreement divides subsidies into three categories. Prohibited subsidies are those that favour the use of domestic over imported inputs or that are targeted at exporters. Actionable subsidies are all others that can be proven to have a negative effect on the trade of another member. Nonactionable subsidies are exempt from WTO discipline and include disadvantaged region initiatives, research and development support, and environmental programs, although this category lapsed in 1999 and members have been unable to agree on its reinstatement (Marsden, 2005). The greatest distinction between prohibited and actionable subsidies is that prohibited subsidies are a violation per se of the SCM while actionable subsidies require a demonstration of adverse effects. Before 1994, the backbone of international subsidies discipline was Article XVI of the GATT, which did not prohibit subsidization but rather developed a framework for disclosure and negotiation.[3] In theory, the SCM's subsidy classification typology is a significant step towards much greater subsidy discipline because most forms of subsidization fall into the second category, leaving a wide number of interventionist practices open to legal challenge. But, in practice, policymakers in this area are unlikely concerned with the new rules because most state aid is not on the chopping block. Research and development programs, environmental and regional development programs, not to mention defence contracts, are all areas in which state support is not affected by the Agreement on Subsidies and Countervailing Measures.

The public policy rationale for industrial subsidization has evolved over the past century, reflecting shifts in economic thought and in the international policy environment. Before World War II, subsidies were part of the beggar-thy-neighbour trade policies of the interwar period (Eichengreen & Irwin, 1993). After the war, Keynesian economic thought emphasized the macroeconomic effects of subsidization for reducing unemployment and spurring economic growth. During this time, the idea that government had a valid, useful role in industry became widely accepted (Hausmann & Rodrik, 2002). This idea is one of the major contributions of Keynesianism, and it has not been displaced by neo-liberal economic thought.

The goal of subsidies discipline is to lessen the distorting impact of domestic support on international trade, thereby raising current levels of international trade and stimulating economic growth. Yet there remains much disagreement among economists on the relationship between trade openness and growth. Although many economists such as David Dollar and Aart Kraay of the World Bank insist that trade openness is itself a propellant of prosperity, a number remain unconvinced.[4] Baldwin (2003) surveyed a number of multi-country case studies that compared international economic policies and rate of economic growth. Most economists agree, he concluded, that some degree of openness is beneficial for economic growth.

Economists disagree, however, on how much public support is required for sustainable growth. Rodriguez and Rodrik (2001) show that open trade policies by themselves are no guarantee of faster growth. Data on global poverty trends supports this research, suggesting that open trade policies may have little to do with growth in certain instances. Empirical data collected by Rodrik (2001) supports this conclusion. Industrialized countries developed behind tariff barriers and have continued to use various non-tariff measures to compete internationally, as have the most recently developed nations, the so-called "Asian tigers" such as Hong Kong, Singapore, South Korea, and Taiwan. Robert Wade (1989) has argued successfully that contrary to neoclassical economic theory, these newly industrialized countries used protection to improve innovation and international competitiveness, as all industrialized nations have done. The goal of WTO law is to regulate the use of protectionist instruments because it remains unclear in the literature to what extent these measures can be an effective and efficient part of national development strategies.[5]

In an open economy with little state intervention, trade may even contribute to growing levels of inequality. In a groundbreaking study of global poverty, Milanovic (2005) pinpoints three main contributors to rising inequality since the late 1980s. The first is rising income differences between the wealthiest urban income earners in OECD countries and the poorest rural incomes in populous Asian countries. The second cause of rising inequality is the pulling ahead of wealthy urban Chinese vis-à-vis poor and rural Chinese and Indian populations. He finds that, measured against urban incomes in China and the developed world, rural incomes are falling behind, due in large part to structural adjustment policies that curbed the redistributive role of the state. The third contribution is the impact these factors have had on national income averages in a comparative context. Milanovic concludes that the past 40 years have seen a hollowing out of the global middle class. The number of very rich and very poor countries has increased significantly in the past 40 years. In 1960, there were 41 rich countries, 19 of which were non-Western. By 2000, there were 31 rich countries, and only 9 were non-Western. In 1980, there were 13 American billionaires. In 2002, there were 374. Over the same period, the average net worth of individuals on the Forbes 400 list grew from $390 million to $2.8 billion.[6]

Getting rich has less to do with free trade and more to do with how firms trade. The world's wealthy nations got rich by backing national firms aggressively and pursuing explicitly mercantilist objectives. Today, many experts now agree that rising levels of global trade are the result of rising levels of economic development — not the engine of growth itself (Stiglitz & Charlton, 2004). This places the subsidies issue in an ambiguous position. Are subsidies to exporters an unfair advantage or a necessary prerequisite for economic growth? At the OECD, for example, there has been a recognition of the value of state support for key sectors of the economy, especially in areas where public sector financing is required to develop high value-added industry. Nevertheless, high levels of subsidization remain the prerogative of developed states with large financial resources.

REGIONAL JETS, GLOBAL COMPETITION

As a trade dependent nation, the Canadian economy relies upon the success of its exporters, and government support has always been central to Canada's success in global markets. Anticipating the policy implications of strategic trade theory, Laura D'Andrea Tyson (1992) asks, when is free trade not the best policy? Her answer is when it hurts strategic industries, such as the aircraft industry, in which investment delivers a higher rate of return than in other sectors. "Indeed, the industry is widely regarded as the best example of an industry in which strategic, beggar-thy-neighbor, rent-shifting policies may improve national economic welfare" (p. 160). Tyson suggests that policymakers pursue a program of "selective reciprocity," in which national trade laws are used to deter and compensate for harmful foreign practices. Trade policy should be used to pry open foreign markets when possible and to protect domestic interests when this is not possible. Non-tariff barriers may be necessary to protect domestic industry from the predatory practices of protectionist nations because the protectionist policies of foreign governments (such as the use of export subsidies) can harm national interests by "shifting industries with high returns and beneficial externalities away from domestic producers and domestic production locations" (p. 3). This is precisely what occurred when Brazil's Embraer tried to take away Bombardier's market share in the lucrative market for regional jets.

Canada has maintained a positive trade balance in aerospace products and services over the past decade.[7] All aerospace industries are heavily subsidized, and it is widely recognized that trade must be underwritten by public funds because the market risks and long-term loan repayment rates typical of aerospace research and development are prohibitive for private capital. In the United States, large exporters such as Boeing have been supported through heavy government investment in research and development, large military contracts, and state tax breaks. Similarly, Airbus receives numerous research and development grants and relies heavily on "launch aid," a system by which member governments subsidize the design and production of new aircraft (Alden & Minder, 2004).

Along with automobile production, aerospace has been the backbone of central Canadian manufacturing, employing approximately 80,000 workers in 2004.[8] This high-tech sector is Canada's single most profitable employer with gross sales approaching C$22 billion per year. This is a fraction of what the United States and the European Union make from the aerospace industry, but it is large enough to make Canada the third largest aerospace manufacturing country in the world. Of those sales, almost C$17 billion comes from exports, approximately 80 per cent of production. In comparison, the US aerospace industry generated US$161 billion in sales in 2004 (Napier, 2005). The EU industry generated €74.6 billion in total sales, with 53 per cent of that going to exports in 2002. Comparatively, the Canadian industry is more dependent upon exports than either the US or the EU aerospace industry, and more dependent upon the development, production, and sale of civil aircraft, whereas the other players have well-developed military

---

Figure 4.1. *State Support for the Aerospace Industry in Canada*

Defence Production Sharing Agreement (1956) – Following World War II, Canada's spending on national defence was not large enough to support a significant aerospace research and development program, so the federal government entered into this agreement with the United States to provide the Canadian industry with general access to US Department of Defense procurement.

Defence Industry Productivity Program (1982–1995) – Before it was dissolved following Canada's entry into the World Trade Organization, the DIPP gave more than C$245 million in grants to Bombardier and a number of sizeable grants and loans to Bombardier subsidiaries de Havilland and Canadair.

Technology Partnerships Canada (TCP) – The TPC is a special operating agency of Industry Canada with a mandate to provide funding support in the preproduction phase for high-tech products with "economic, social, and environmental benefits to Canadians." The aerospace industry has been one of the largest recipients of government funding through this mechanism.

Export Development Canada (EDC) – This Crown corporation provides trade finance services (such as insurance and loans) to Canadian exporters. Over the past two decades, EDC has held an aerospace portfolio worth more than C$9 billion.

- The Canada Account is a portion of EDC capital that is used to support export transactions that the Minister of International Trade deems to be in the national interest. These transactions are negotiated, executed, and administered through EDC, but all risks are assumed by the federal government.

Sources: Technology Partnerships Canada, Export Development Canada.

---

industries. Aerospace also accounts for a higher portion of Canada's GDP (1.84 per cent) than does the sector in the United States (1.47 per cent) or the European Union (0.85 per cent).

Support for Canadian aerospace giant Bombardier includes design, production, and export-oriented support. Before its dismantling in 1995, the Defence Industry Productivity Program helped support Bombardier. In the past 15 years, Bombardier has received state support through an arranged buyout of government owned Canadair, makers of corporate and, later, regional jets, as well as through loans from Technology Partnerships Canada (TPC) and airplane financing deals through the Canada Account of Export Development Canada (EDC). It is impossible to know precisely how much support Bombardier has received. Ottawa has provided funding to the aerospace industry in the ballpark of $10 billion over the past several decades (see Figure 4.1 on the previous page). As Canada's national champion, the lion's share has gone to Bombardier—of that there is no doubt. Embraer gets a similar level of support from Brazil, with most state funds directed towards an export-financing program designed to counteract the financing disadvantages experienced by southern exporters.

Brazil—Export Financing Program for Aircraft

After acquiring Canadair in 1986, Bombardier followed through on a project to "stretch" several business jet models currently produced by Canadair into 50- to 70-seat regional jets, the first of their type on the market. Trade Partnerships Canada provided C$87 million in the form of an interest-free loan to begin development. By 1989, Brazil was also reworking the designs for its business jets, preparing to compete with Bombardier in the lucrative new market for regional jets. For the first half of the 1990s, Bombardier was the only supplier of regional jets in the world. But, in the spring of 1996, Embraer landed a deal with Continental Airlines for 25 regional jets, with the option to purchase up to 175 more. Embraer's price for the jets (including financing) was approximately US$14.5 million, well below the US$18 million price of a Bombardier model (Hadekel, 2004, p. 193).

In June of 1996, Canada sued Brazil over its export credit program. Brazil countersued, and two relatively small aircraft manufacturers opened the door to judicial scrutiny of one of the most protected and sensitive sectors of their national economies. The Programa de Financiamento às Exportações (PROEX) is an export development program that provides export credits to Brazilian exporters through direct financing and interest rate equalization payments. The payments were designed to bring the cost of financing Brazilian exports down to international levels. The cost of financing an Embraer jet was reduced by approximately US$2.5 million over the service life of the plane, according to Canadian estimates. When the Brazilian government decided to finance an aircraft transaction, PROEX lent a portion of the funds required through interest equalization payments in the form of national treasury grants to lending agencies. These grants, in the form of government bonds, cover the difference between the amount of interest paid by the purchaser on the transaction and the cost to the lending agency of raising the funds.

PROEX provides foreign purchasers of Embraer aircraft with interest rate subsidies designed to make Brazilian exports more competitive. It is widely recognized in the heavily subsidized aerospace industry that aircraft manufacturers are selling not only planes but also purchase financing. PROEX interest rate subsidies are valued at 3.5 to 3.8 percentage points per annum over a ten-year period, effectively lowering the cost of financing for Embraer aircraft below market rates, which hover above 4 per cent. PROEX payments, made to the lending institution in the form of national treasury bonds (Notas do Tesouro Nacional–Série 1) known as NTN-1 bonds, are redeemable on a semi-annual basis from the Brazilian Tesouro Nacional, or they can be discounted for a lump sum on the open market.

Brazilian exports financed on international markets compete at a disadvantage because they are unable to obtain optimal terms of credit. Similarly, Brazilian banks and the Brazilian government are unable to borrow funds at interest rates as low as banks and governments in industrialized countries obtain, and therefore they are unable to offer competitive loans to the purchasers of Embraer's regional jets. Brazil agreed with Canada that the PROEX interest equalization program was an export subsidy, but it argued that PROEX is exempt from the general prohibition on export subsidies in Article 3.1 of the SCM by virtue of Article 27, which allows special and differential treatment for developing countries. Furthermore, Embraer needed to compete with the substantial subsidies enjoyed by Bombardier. The determination of whether PROEX was used to gain a material advantage in the marketplace should be made by comparing its benefits to the "total package of benefits offered by Canada" (WTO, 1999, para. 4.131). Aircraft manufactures must be competitive not only in the cost of planes but also in the cost of financing because airline business models look at the entire monthly cost of financing an aircraft for a given route.

PROEX offered below market-level financing, which was better than the financing that Canada's public sector lender, Export Development Canada, could offer. In many cases, PROEX grants lowered interest to almost half the current market rates. This, Canada argued, was an anticompetitive strategy aimed at taking market share away from Bombardier rather than at lowering the cost of Brazilian financing for foreign purchasers. In fact, four of the eleven transactions in question were arranged through lending institutions outside Brazil, throwing into question Brazil's stated claim of needing to provide export support in order to counter high interest rates charged by banks financing southern exports, rates dubbed by litigators as "Brazil risk." According to purchasers of Embraer aircraft, one of the key factors in purchasing decisions was the availability of very low financing charges (WTO, 1999, para. 4.46-4.48).

Canada only asked the WTO to rule on the interest equalization component of PROEX. The PROEX program also provided many risk management services very similar to Canada's EDC. Furthermore, Canada did not dispute that Brazil is a developing country entitled to special and differential treatment under Article 27 of the SCM. Article 27 allowed developing nations to phase out export subsidy regimes over eight years, in effect allowing certain subsidy programs to continue in the short term, as long as governments are actively working to end them by the negotiated deadline, December 31, 2002. However, Canada argued that Article 27 only applies in so far as developing countries meet the conditions set out in Article 27.4 — that they are actively phasing out subsidies during the eight years after the SCM entered into force. Brazil must phase out subsidies sooner if they are inconsistent with development needs, as was the case with Embraer, Canada argued, a world-renowned manufacturer of turbo-prop aircraft and regional jets, which has been competing globally for more than 20 years.

The panel decided against Brazil and, in doing so, clarified the responsibilities of developing countries under the Agreement on Subsidies and Countervailing Measures. The panel decided that the burden of proof is on the complaining country to prove that a developing country acted in contravention of SCM Article 27. Canada had argued the opposite, that the burden was on the developing nation to prove that the subsidy was necessary. Score one for Brazil. However, the panel decided that subsidies do not have to be paid out for a benefit to be conferred. This means that the finding of subsidization extended even to the aircraft purchase options negotiated, but not yet paid out, under the PROEX financing scheme. Furthermore, it is possible for a developing country to act in a manner inconsistent with Article 3, despite being covered by Article 27. Special and differential treatment is not a blank cheque; it is only a certain amount of latitude, subject to restrictions. The panel found that Brazil did not comply with the conditions of Article 27 because Canada was able to satisfy the burden of proof that Brazil had increased the amount of its export subsidies. The Appellate Body upheld the decision.

PROEX II and III

A compliance panel was convened less than a year later to determine whether Brazil had changed its financing structure (WTO, 2000, July 21). Brazil had modified its PROEX program (referred to by the panel as PROEX II) so that the interest equalization payments were reduced to an international market benchmark that was higher than the interest charges of the original program. Canada contended that Brazil could not continue to issue NTN-1 bonds for transactions completed before the decision and that the modified payment structure of PROEX II was still an illegal subsidy. The panel agreed on both counts, finding that Brazil was still using PROEX to gain a material advantage in the market for regional jets. The Appellate Body upheld the decision that PROEX II continued to be used to gain a material advantage in civil aviation markets. In arbitration, Canada claimed material injury worth US$480 million. The arbitrator estimated the cost to the Canadian aerospace industry as somewhat lower, allowing Canada to retaliate with C$344.2 million of countervailing measures. It was the largest subsidies decision to date in the international trade regime (WTO, 2000, August 28).

Canada attacked Brazil's use of the PROEX program one more time, in a second set of compliance proceedings (WTO DSB, 2001, July 26). Litigators argued that Brazil's most recent revision of the interest equalization payment scheme was also illegal. Just like PROEX I and II, PROEX III was also a constructed buy-down of interest rates. This time, the panel concluded that PROEX III financing was not inconsistent with SCM Article 3.1, the portion of the agreement that bans subsidies based on export performance. It is legally possible for Brazil to operate PROEX III in such a way that it does not result in a benefit being conferred upon producers of regional aircraft, and the program is therefore not a subsidy.

Canada: Measures Affecting the Export of Civilian Aircraft

Launched shortly after Canada's request for consultations over PROEX, Brazil's suit alleged that Canada had also granted Bombardier export subsidies prohibited under the Agreement on Subsidies and Countervailing Measures. The panel considered claims made by Brazil that the activities of Export Development Canada (EDC), the Canada Account of EDC, the Canada–Quebec Subsidiary Agreements on Industrial Development, the Société de Développement Industriel du Québec (SDI), Technology Partnerships Canada (TPC), and the Defence Industry Productivity Program (DIPP) constituted illegal export subsidies. Further, Brazil alleged that the sale of Ontario's 49 per cent stake in de Havilland to Bombardier was also an actionable subsidy.

The panel found that financing for the export of regional jets through the EDC's Canada Account amounted to an illegal subsidy, as did Trade Partnerships Canada's assistance to the regional aircraft industry, although neither program was inconsistent with the SCM per se. According to the panel, the Canada Account constitutes discretionary legislation and therefore is not a prima facie subsidy. The panel therefore had to look at how the legislation was used. It requested the transaction record for the Canada Account, and Canada refused, disclosing that the account had been used on two occasions for "export transactions" (WTO, 1999a, para. 9.217) but not giving any further details, arguing that to do so would divulge confidential business information. The panel found that there was a prima facie case that the Canada Account debt financing was most likely below market rates and therefore conferred a benefit, contingent upon export.

Technology Partnerships Canada had given tens of millions of dollars to Bombardier, de Havilland, and other aerospace manufacturers. Canada allowed that the TPC program did grant subsidies, arguing that these were not contingent upon export. The panel requested internal TPC project assessments, and, again, Canada did not comply. Litigators explained that these contributions were above C$20 million and required the approval of the federal cabinet. Therefore, all discussed recommendations, options, strategies, and analyses are contained in the "Memoranda to Cabinet." By Canadian constitutional convention, these are cabinet confidences and cannot be divulged. Again, Canada failed to rebut the prima facie case, and TPC assistance to the regional aircraft industry was ruled an illegal subsidy within the meaning of SCM Article 1.1. The Appellate Body report upheld the panel's decision.

When implementing the panel decision, the Canadian government made very few policy changes. It cancelled future funding commitments and suspended 86 applications for funding, pending changes to the rules. Technology Partnerships Canada clarified the nature of its program by modifying it to target research and development rather than product development. Royalty payments are no longer tied to product sales. They are determined by more general measures of company performance and share price. Few changes were made to the Canada Account program. In the compliance phase of panel review, the WTO upheld Canada's changes to TPC and struck down the Canada Account program (Krikorian, 2005). To date, Canada has not complied with the panel ruling on the Canada Account.

Canada — Export Credits and Loan Guarantees for Regional Aircraft

Shortly after Canada was granted leave to retaliate against Brazil's use of PROEX II, Bombardier learned of a new deal in which Embraer was offering its special financing rates to Air Wisconsin Airlines Corporation, in a transaction for 75 jets. In January 2001, Bombardier, with the help of the EDC's Canada Account, offered to match the Embraer financing package. Bombardier took the sale and Brazil sued. With the suit well underway, Canada disclosed that it had also used the same tactic to secure a contract with Northwest Airlines in July of the same year for up to 150 aircraft.

Canada argued that Canada Account financing should be legal because it fell within the exception in Annex I (k-2) of the SCM Agreement, which allowed export credit practices that conform to the provisions in the "OECD Arrangement." The OECD Arrangement sets out the commercial interest reference rates (CIRR), a set of minimum interest rates that should be offered by an OECD member involved in export credit financing transactions. The panel upheld Brazil's claim that the financing deals for Air Wisconsin were prohibited export subsidies. In doing so, it set a higher standard for subsidy matching deals than that of the CIRR.[9] At the end of the 90-day compliance period, Canada informed the membership of the Dispute

Settlement Body that it had not taken action and would not take action with regard to any of the transactions found to be inconsistent with its obligations under the SCM Agreement (WTO, 2002, May 24).

In arbitration, Brazil was authorized to implement countervailing measures of almost US$248 million, a larger amount than the arbitrator's calculation of the value of Bombardier's subsidy because of Canada's stated intention not to comply with the panel's ruling (WTO, 2003, February 17). The Brazilian award effectively cancelled Canada's earlier award, leaving bilateral talks as the only alternative for settling the dispute. Unsurprisingly, bilateral talks have not produced an agreement on aircraft financing, and both states continue to support their aerospace industries aggressively.

INDUSTRIAL STRATEGY AND TRADE GOVERNANCE

One of the key reasons that members consider the juridical and binding nature of dispute settlement to be a valuable aspect of the new system is that it is less politically contentious in many cases than are bilateral concessions. The growth of international judicial bodies over the past five decades has been phenomenal. Since the end of World War II, 17 international judicial bodies and several dozen quasi-judicial bodies have been created.[10] These institutions adjudicate an increasing number of international issues, from trade to border disputes and even disputes involving ocean resources, which are taken to the International Tribunal for the Law of the Sea, a standing dispute settlement court which has adjudicated 13 cases since it entered into force in 1994.[11] Dispute settlement mechanisms take some of the guesswork out of foreign policy strategies because they help to clarify the rules around an increasing number of big issues.

Most trade experts agree that the WTO's dispute settlement mechanism has been a step forward for international trade regulation because members believe it to be more effective than the GATT system. The subsidy dispute between Canada and Brazil is only one of a growing number of cases that defies this popular perception. As we saw in the softwood dispute, one case seems likely to beget another at times. In fact, Alter (2003) has argued that current mechanisms to decide disputes may generate as much conflict as they resolve. It is not clear from the empirical data whether nations actually launch retaliatory panels or whether the WTO has simply become the first recourse after the failure of bilateral mechanisms.

In this case, Canada decided not to comply with the panel's final ruling, claiming that Brazil had not complied fully with earlier panel decisions and therefore government considered compliance to be contrary to Canada's national interest — a rationale implicitly articulated in Canada's terse note to the arbitrator prior to his levying of penalties in the dispute entitled

"Canada–Export Credits and Loan Guarantees for Regional Aircraft." Non-compliance seemed to be part of a larger strategy that took into consideration the fact that Canada had already won a non-compliance award against Brazil. This meant that Canada could protect privileged cabinet-level information at little or no cost because its non-compliance penalty would be cancelled out by Brazil's.

The paradox of dispute settlement is that, on the one hand, the system attempts to lift interstate relations out of power politics and into a juridical arena, but, on the other, it relies on state power to enforce panel decisions (van den Broek, 2003). Although dispute settlement based upon the rule of law ameliorates the advantage of market power in theory, in fact, it places this power at the heart of the panel process. Nevertheless, use of retaliatory measures in the dispute settlement process is rare, with only the United States and the European Union undertaking such measures successfully (Lawrence, 2003). Retaliation is difficult for small countries because the economic and diplomatic costs are greater than the benefits. One reason that retaliation rates remain low and compliance rates seem to be high is that most states recognize that dispute settlement is part of the trade game. In the high-stakes political economy of technology trade, the WTO has quickly become yet another variable in the game of global competition.

Export subsidies have long been a strategic part of international trade competition, and they continue to have real, if incalculable, impacts on the domestic economies of trade partners. Recent attempts by Canada to negotiate looser terms for subsidy discipline show that policymakers recognize that support for exports is often required in order to compete successfully in highly competitive international markets for high-tech products (Magnus, 2004). Competition between rival centres of production drove Brazil to lower the price of Embraer aircraft financing to the point at which Embraer could undercut Bombardier and shore up its market presence. This type of competition is not sustainable indefinitely, but it did work long enough for Brazil to gain its objective: a place in the regional jet market for Embraer. That Canada and Brazil chose to enter bilateral negotiations rather than implement retaliatory measures emphasizes the complex relationship between industrial organization, national regulation, and trade policy—a sensitive matrix in which freer trade must be negotiated rather than litigated.

WTO litigation has led to a marginal tightening of discipline for aerospace funding but not to a change in the institutional and programmatic approach that drives Canada's industrial support for the aerospace sector. Technology Partnerships Canada replaced the Defence Industry Productivity Program in 1995. It was created to be a WTO compliant mechanism for the precompetitive state support of Canada's fledgling high-tech industries.

Aerospace now has to share government largesse with environmental firms and biotechnology companies. The SCM Agreement states that no more than 33 per cent of the funding for research, development, and production can come from government. In recent years, this cap has been raised to 40 per cent. Policymakers eventually skirted WTO rules by deciding that repayment of TPC loans would be based on the overall success of the company, rather than taking the form of royalties on product sales, which were ruled to be an export subsidy (Hadekel, 2004, p. 171).

Ultimately, the WTO ruling affected the institutional mechanisms Canada used to implement its industrial strategy — but not the strategy itself. A significant outcome of membership has been that WTO dispute settlement has changed the way that Canada solves complex subsidy disputes. In the past, the largest emphasis had been on a diplomatic solution to trade remedy disputes. The judicialization of the international trade regime allows Canada to use litigation as one of the primary strategies to solve disputes. Canada has much experience and a deep well of resources and knowledge that facilitate this type of dispute settlement.

CONCLUSION: THE NETWORK OF BARGAINS

Two prominent relationships can be highlighted in this network of bargains. The first is the relationship between governments. Although these cases did not do lasting damage to Canada's relations with Brazil, they did highlight the way in which trade litigation and the high politics of interstate relations go hand in hand. They also illustrate the way that governments pull out all the stops to protect the market share of a national champion. This brings us to our second relationship, that of governments with domestic firms. The federal government's relationship with Bombardier goes far beyond its relations with other aerospace firms. Bombardier is a national champion, which means that government has invested much in its success.

Bombardier provides well-paying jobs for thousands of people in and around Montreal and across central Canada. De Havilland Canada, located in the north end of Toronto, is a subsidiary of Bombardier. One line of jets is partly assembled at de Havilland's Downsview plant, and the "green airplane" — an aircraft that has engines, flight controls, and little else — is flown to Montreal where its interior is finished according to the specifications of the buyer. Companies across Canada subcontract with Bombardier. In short, Bombardier is not only a lynchpin in Canada's high-tech sector but also a symbol of the dynamism of the Canadian economy. Other examples of national champions include General Motors in the United States, Airbus in Europe, and perhaps Toyota in Japan.

Two conclusions should be drawn from this discussion of subsidy litigation in Canada's high-tech civil aircraft industry. First, dispute settlement is not effective when Canada faces an opponent with which it has few trade ties. Realistically, this means not only that litigation is ineffective with Canada's major trading partner, the United States, because of the massive economic disparities between the two countries, but also that it is ineffective with Canada's other partners because Canada lacks the economic leverage to enforce compliance at the WTO. Seen from another perspective, we could argue that the WTO has been successful in bringing parties together and sending them to the bargaining table. However, in this case, Canada and Brazil have been unable to come to an acceptable arrangement. Both tweaked their subsidy mechanisms in order to stay on the right side of the SCM Agreement, but, in practice, both continue to subsidize their aerospace industries.

In a countermovement, the judicialization of dispute settlement seems to have directed Canada's trade conflict resolution strategies towards litigation. A better way to describe this dynamic would be to say that, even though dispute settlement brings parties together and encourages a bilateral diplomatic solution, it seems to have become something of a mechanism of "first resort." There seems to be little reason for states not to make good use of legal channels that have been put in place to ease trade frictions, but, if Alter (2003) is correct in her argument that dispute settlement may exacerbate conflict, then the judicial angle should be approached with caution. In the final balance, Canada has swapped older, and sometimes ineffective, diplomatic dispute settlement processes for a system that has not produced appreciably better outcomes. All states recognize that strategic industrial sectors require government intervention to balance public and private sector needs. As global trade continues to expand, members are not phasing out subsidies. Members may modify subsidization policies in order to appear to meet the terms of WTO law, but they continue to use state support in new and sophisticated ways to compete effectively in strategic markets.

Notes

1. Krugman (1994) argues that countries do not compete in the same way that corporations do. Corporations may compete for a single market, but countries are more complex. Their firms may sell some products that compete, but they are also "each other's main export markets and each other's main suppliers of useful imports." A misplaced focus on competitiveness obscures a more complex empirical argument—that, as is the case of the United States, a trade surplus may be a sign of national weakness, a deficit a sign of global confidence in the overall dynamism

of the hegemon's economy. Nevertheless, Tyson's definition of competitiveness works well for a small, open economy with a greater reliance on exports, such as Canada's.

2. The full text of the Agreement on Subsidies and Countervailing measures can be found in the *Agreement Establishing the World Trade Organization Annex 1a: Multilateral Agreements on Trade in Goods — Agreement on Subsidies and Countervailing Measures*, which is available on the World Trade Organization website at http://www.wto.org/english/docs_e/legal_e/24-scm_01_e.htm.

3. Paragraph four states, "Further, as from 1 January 1958 or the earliest practicable date thereafter, contracting parties shall cease to grant either directly or indirectly any form of subsidy on the export of any product other than a primary product which subsidy results in the sale of such product for export at a price lower than the comparable price charged for the like product to buyers in the domestic market. Until 31 December 1957 no contracting party shall extend the scope of any such subsidization beyond that existing on 1 January 1955 by the introduction of new, or the extension of existing, subsidies."

4. For a debate on the role of trade in economic growth, see David Dollar and Aart Kraay (2001). For a cogent critique of their position, see Dani Rodrik (2000).

5. Key to the issue of growth and subsidization is the question of the impact of subsidies on domestic prices. Economists cannot agree on how to measure the effect of subsidies on the price of goods. The OECD has attempted to measure the rate of subsidization in member economies, and statistics such as the producer support estimate (PSE) are internationally recognized as the most accurate representations to date. But even this scale does not provide an adequate measure of price change under subsidization.

6. According to Merrill Lynch's *World Wealth Report* of 2005, the "ultrarich," defined as individuals with a net worth over $30 million, now number about 50,000 worldwide (Capgemini US LCC, 2005). The result of this unprecedented mushrooming of personal wealth has been the growth, especially in the United States, of a luxury service industry targeted at this lucrative segment of the market. Negotiating aircraft leases, purchasing art, managing estates, and securing the services of public-relations specialists are all part of a day's work for a new cadre of lifestyle management experts (Kolhatkar, 2006). Unlike other fads of conspicuous consumption, it is expected that this new class of servant is here to stay.

7. Interestingly, one of the newest players in Canada's aerospace industry is the province of Prince Edward Island. Aerospace is now the province's third largest industry, with production worth C$300 million annually and a workforce of 800 employees. See www.apei.ca for more information on PEI's new high-tech economy.

8. The US industry employed approximately 584,000 workers in 2004, and the EU industry employed 408,000 in 2002, the most recent industry figures. Figures are

available from the Aerospace Industries Association at www.aia-aerospace.org and the European Association of Aerospace Industries at www.aecma.org.

9. The OECD responded to the panel's decision by amending its provisions to comply with the ruling. It also explicitly incorporated its matching program into the OECD Arrangement so that there would be no confusion that greater state flexibility in this area was essential. See Krikorian (2005, pp. 932–933).

10. See Cesare Romano (1999). See also the Project on International Courts and Tribunals. This organization has developed a synoptic chart of every international tribunal at work today, covering the waterfront of international criminal law, human rights, trade law, regional integration, and monitoring bodies for many different administrative and legal purposes. The chart is available at www. pict-pcti.org/publications/synoptic_chart.html.

11. See the tribunal's website at www.itlos.org for more information on this emerging issue in global governance.

CHAPTER FIVE

Intellectual Property, National Treatment, and Trade in Cultural Goods: The Case of Split-Run Magazines

This chapter deals with the contentious issue of applying existing trade agreements to areas of commerce that are rising in importance but for which there is little precedent in the history of GATT regulation. This discussion, more so than the three previous case studies, engages with the difficult intersection between trade and the "soft law" of human rights—in this case, cultural rights. International legal scholars make the distinction between hard law, in which the rights and obligations of states are clearly identified, and soft law, in which obligations are more ambiguous or international standards are impossible to enforce with any precision. So-called soft law deals with aspects of the regulation of international migration, environmental protection, and the protection of cultural rights, for example. Culture is a particularly difficult area of international rule making because global flows of cultural goods and services affect a number of economic sectors. Furthermore, cultural goods are never only products to be bought and sold on the open market. They are also powerful symbols and representations of ethnic, national, and religious identities.

The last two decades have witnessed a broadening and deepening of global cultural flows that is unprecedented in history. Thanks to new information technologies, a worldwide audience consumes cultural products such as movies, television programs, and music. Magazines, books, and newspapers are sold around the globe. Important members at the WTO are leading the program to broaden and deepen market access for cultural property across the globe—especially in relation to entertainment and media industries. At the same time, many academics and policy analysts are rethinking the challenges posed by cultural diversity, as trade in cultural goods and services has been a key driver behind the intensification of global flows of people, capital, and ideas (UNESCO, 2000). Canada's magazine case is especially important because it caused Canada to re-evaluate its commitment to a single regulatory framework for global trade in cultural goods.

The first section of this chapter examines Canada's trade in cultural goods as it relates to WTO law. The central policy trade-off in the regulation of cultural trade is between that of "protecting creations and inventions of the mind and disseminating these creations for the broader good of society" (Doern & Sharaput, 2000, p. 19). In Canada, contentious dispute settlement decisions are a key factor in determining government's recent stand on the issue of cultural pluralism in an era of global intellectual property protection. The second section examines the WTO's dispute settlement record in the cultural sphere, which necessarily requires a closer look at the Agreement on Trade-Related Aspects of Intellectual Property Rights (TRIPs). Up to now, only a few cases have been brought to the WTO that deal specifically with cultural products, and most of those have been TRIPs enforcement proceedings launched by the United States. A notable exception is Canada's dispute with the United States over split-run magazines, which was a market access case litigated under GATT Articles III and XI.

The split-run magazines case is perhaps the most important cultural dispute at the WTO to date because it dealt with the important issue of cultural content. Panellists were asked to decide upon the contentious question of what makes a cultural commodity different from any other tradeable good. Previously, the GATT had dodged this bullet by providing exemptions for cultural commodities. The WTO did not accept Canada's argument that news magazines have a cultural value separate from their economic value. In fact, Article XX of the GATT, which provides exemptions on the basis of biodiversity, natural resource conservation, and the protection of national artefacts, has never been used successfully to protect cultural diversity. What is most troubling is that WTO agreements contain no effective solution to the problems that surround the provision of cultural goods through commercial trade.

The third section examines the ways in which the globalization of digital technology is changing the playing field for civil society and WTO governance alike. I conclude with a brief discussion of Canada's policy shift—from pursuing a cultural exemption at the WTO to supporting, and indeed providing, a driving force for the development of a new international instrument for cultural diversity at UNESCO.[1] The United Nations has shown a greater sensitivity to local and regional cultural diversity in the face of multinational media dominance. The network of bargains in this case contains a particularly dense overlap of governmental, industry, and citizen interests.

Canadians also began to organize citizens in Europe and Asia and their respective governments. The International Network for Cultural Diversity (INCD) was a Canadian initiative to bring together artists and concerned citizens from around the world in a call for cultural diversity in an era of globalization. The INCD's statement of principles asserts that "the fruits of artistic creation are more than conventional goods and services, each is unique and all are an integral part of human societies."[2] This statement is a direct response to the magazine case that treated Canadian and American cultural goods as directly substitutable. Whereas the INCD is a non-governmental organization aimed at citizens, the International Network on Cultural Policy (INCP) is an intergovernmental initiative aimed at bringing together diverse national governments with an interest in "advocating for and building international consensus around the promotion of cultural diversity."[3] Also begun as a Canadian initiative in 1998, INCP currently includes 39 ministers of culture and remains one of the most important venues for the discussion of emerging cultural policy issues.

This shift from inside to outside the WTO is a significant feature of the cultural trade story with a potentially large effect on the Canadian cultural economy — in terms of both regulation and future negotiations at the WTO around trade in cultural goods and services. Is Canada at the forefront of a global drive for a less rigid, more culturally sensitive form of trade regulation, or is this a bid to shield domestic industry in the face of stiff American competition? It is likely a little bit of both.

NEW INTELLECTUAL PROPERTY RULES AND CANADA'S CULTURAL INDUSTRIES

Culture is a difficult and elusive term to define. Researchers and social thinkers have used hundreds of definitions of culture. Always, definitions of the term say more about the cultural context of the thinker than they do about the thing itself, as Stanley (2005) points out. Drache and Froese (2006) define culture as a set of ideas and practices embedded in the plural and diverse historical experience of a society. Culture is central to social relations and building cohesive societies because it intersects with closely held social values, public perceptions, and popular sovereignty. It is so complex because it is a tradeable commodity, a tool of identity for groups and individuals, and a strategic resource for national societies. More than ever, culture has become a tool of identity, used by states and citizens to defend sovereignty and further national goals. Yet, at the same time that the forces of globalization have brought the twin concerns of cultural identity and pluralism to the forefront of the global public debate, they have also spotlighted the increasing profitability of cultural trade and the attendant challenges of enforcing intellectual property (IP) rights.

Social scientists have long been interested in the relationship between culture and economics.[4] But what makes any systematic examination of culture so difficult is the conceptual divide between cultural value and economic value. Throsby (2001) suggests that the main reason for this difficulty is that economists take the individual as the primary unit of analysis while any analysis of culture must begin at the group or collective level. As a result, economists throughout the twentieth century have had little to say about the conceptual relationship between the idea of economic value, regulated by supply and demand, and the idea of cultural value, which is a reflection of a collective identity.

With the rise of a comprehensive set of intellectual property rules comes the prospect of increasing trade integration in the cultural sphere. New ideas about international economic integration bring with them renewed interest in the relationship between economics and culture and a new understanding of the centrality of culture, in terms of both economic growth in the developing world and economic outcomes in industrialized nations. This rediscovery of the complex relationship between economics and culture is in part due to a renewed interest on the part of political scientists and social theorists about the role of culture in shaping market institutions, public policy priorities, and economic growth trajectories.

In all member countries, domestic cultural producers compete with imported cultural goods, often from the United States. Although American films may dominate in many markets, countries never rely entirely on foreign producers for the cultural products they consume. In Canada, a jurisdiction long regarded by Hollywood as part of the domestic market, audiences and governments regard local filmmaking as an exercise in cultural sovereignty — as being about the construction of identity as much as it is about producing a tradeable commodity. Bear in mind that cultural goods, by their very nature, never conform to the standard neoclassical economic account of comparative advantage for two reasons. First, books, music, and films are not like other products, which are produced and then consumed. Cultural goods are never fully consumed in the cultural experience. In fact, thanks to the Internet, these goods tend to multiply in digital form; effortless multiplication (think file sharing) drives down their price, much to the dismay of producers. Second, cultural goods are qualitatively incomparable with other commodities because the value of culture is related to its intangible characteristics, not its physical characteristics. A spoon is a spoon, no matter where it is produced in the world. In qualitative terms, an American film is not a Swedish film. There is a difference that matters very much to both connoisseur and casual consumer alike.

Interestingly, treating films like spoons in the global marketplace can have unforeseen consequences. Imagine if a single firm based in South Africa produced half the world's supply of spoons. This firm made dozens of different styles of spoons and sold them in many regional markets, from Shanghai to Sydney to South Bend, Indiana. The fact that half the world's spoons were being supplied by a single producer would have no impact on the quality of the spoons sold, per se. Nor would the material used to make the spoons necessarily offend regional sensibilities. Chances are the average person would little care about the faceless corporation that facilitated the worldwide transfer of soup from bowl to mouth. The same is not true for cultural products. A spoon purchased in North America is not likely to be made in North America, but the same is never true of cultural goods. A Chinese film is not an American film, nor is it likely ever to be mistaken as such.

Peter Grant (2004) describes how, when traditional market models are applied to trade in culture, the "blockbuster effect" often chokes creativity and ultimately starves the market of diverse cultural products. If one firm made half the world's spoons, most people would not notice, unless they were advised by a banker to invest in spoons! But if one company made half the world's films, we would all notice, and most of us would be a little concerned. This example is extreme, but current models for investing in media have a tendency to guide the flow of investment dollars toward "sure bets." Media companies bet on the cultural product that will guarantee the fastest profits, such as blockbuster movies and pop music hits. Producers profit from economies of scale at home and reap massive gains from entertainment markets abroad — albeit at a discounted rate due to sophisticated counterfeiting rings in Asia. The goal is to create a virtuous circle linking localized production, global distribution, and the cosmopolitan consumer — an integrated, global commodity chain for culture.[5] Film investors do not necessarily care about the health of diverse markets for local films from Quebec to New Delhi. They care about safe investments that reap large profits. According to the principles of rational investment, money should flow towards cultural products that turn a profit, but, if cultural policy were left entirely to the market, valuable cultural voices would surely be lost forever.

Three models of cultural policy have been delineated, developed, and debated by governments concerned with the future of multiculturalism. Canada, the United States and the European Union have contrasting and competing views on the role of the state in cultural protection and promotion. The European Union looks to build linkages and networks between state regulatory policy and cultural producers. This tripartite approach is difficult at the best of times, but has been quite effective nonetheless. Iapadre and Formentini (2005) show that the creation of a common market has reduced the trade-offs between integration and cultural policies because the removal of trade barriers has been used as a tool to promote cultural pluralism by enlarging market access for audiovisual products. The European Union is linguistically and socially diverse, and its internal stability depends upon a pluralistic approach to the global commons. It regards freedom of expression as important to protect as part of its commitment to the social market. The European Union is very proactive at the supranational level. Its social democratic stance is that culture is a public good to be nurtured, much like the environment, for its 450 million citizens.

The Anglo-American model is sharply contrasting in its regulatory and market dimensions. It should be noted that, despite the fact that Great Britain is a member of the European Union, its elites share many ideas with their American counterparts. Simply, this model views diversity as a function of competition and not the other way around. Consumers choose their cultural diet from a buffet of options. And as with many buffets, portion size is more important than quality and breadth of choice. The Anglo-American model requires supersize profits and relies on regulators to create an environment conducive to corporate growth. American media conglomerates are promoting aggressively the US State Department's objectives to broaden copyright law and deepen trade liberalization. In contrast, policymakers in the European Union understand that the culture-trade interface cannot be one-dimensional, and trade must accommodate diversity, not the other way around (Charnovitz, 2005).

The model that Canada has pioneered is one of public-private partnerships with a large role for public broadcasters and an even larger role for private actors. This model is predicated upon a large internal market for cultural products. For example, in Canada's robust publishing industry, Canadian publishers produce around 85 per cent of the titles available in Canada. Nevertheless, they only account for about half of all book sales (Lorimer, 1996). Canadian consumers spend hundreds of millions of dollars a year on books, but clearly many favour such American publishing blockbusters as *The Da Vinci Code*.

It has always been this way in Canada. In the film industry, Hollywood considers Canada to be part of its domestic market, and Canada's entertainment market is more highly saturated by American films than is any other national market in the world. By the early 1990s, American films captured 96 per cent of the market; Canadian films held a paltry 2 per cent of theatre attendance receipts (Magder, 1996). Proximity to the American cultural juggernaut has fundamentally shaped Canadian cultural policy, turning it away from the European model of protection and promotion favoured by the Massey Report of 1951 and forging a hybrid model that preserves a larger role for private sector actors. Dorland (1996) notes that in every case, the mission of Canadian public policy has been to support, not to obstruct, the growth of the private production in the cultural industries. As a result, public broadcasting in Canada has always been an enclave in a larger industry. Compare Canada's niche role for public broadcasting with the leading position of the BBC in Britain. The Canadian Broadcasting Corporation is not as well funded as its European counterparts, yet it offers a more robust public alternative than is available in the United States.

The model is held together through a program of public advocacy and accountability that often promises more than it delivers. Nevertheless, its main feature is not a diminished public sector but rather a double movement between privatization and increased public presence. Public broadcasting has been forced, over the past two decades, to look to private companies for more and more of its production needs, and the previous Liberal government cut $500 million from the Canadian Broadcasting Corporation's budget, dramatically weakening the national broadcaster. At the same time, however, the film and print industries are increasingly reliant on public funds. Federal spending on culture has been growing by about 2 per cent per year, and provincial and municipal expenditures have been increasing even faster, by 4 per cent and 7 per cent, respectively (Statistics Canada, 2005).

Canadians are consuming more cultural products than ever before. In an ongoing project measuring flows of cultural goods into and out of Canada, Statistics Canada found that Canadian trade in cultural goods has grown steadily over the past decade.[6] Exports of Canadian cultural products have doubled since 1996, and imports of media and entertainment from other countries have also grown by 25 per cent. By 2004, Canada's culture industries exported $2.4 billion in media and entertainment products, most of them destined for consumption in the United States. In turn, Canadians bought more than $4.4 billion in foreign cultural products. Canada imports far more entertainment from the United States than it sells to the entire world combined, running an annual trade deficit in cultural product of approximately $2 billion. In addition, Canadians buy more cultural products now than at any time in the past. However, the most important fact to note is that our appetite for foreign products has not diminished the market for home-grown cultural products. Magazines are the best barometers of national cultural consumption because they are produced almost exclusively for local consumption. Canadian publishers of periodicals have had banner years recently. Magazine profits are up, and industry revenues topped $1.6 billion — this despite increased competition from American split runs and online content.

DISPUTES INVOLVING CULTURAL PRODUCTS AT THE WTO

Litigation at the WTO has been a preferred method for harmonizing national copyright standards in the hyper-competitive music, film, and television industries. One of the putative aims of the current round of trade negotiations is to stamp out the piracy of information. In the TRIPs framework, all members of the WTO are obligated to provide national treatment for all sound recordings and to provide criminal penalties for piracy. Under TRIPs, copyright is protected for 50 years from the date of production, a much longer period than many national laws stipulated. For example, under Japanese law in the mid-1990s, sound recordings were only protected for 25 years. Japan was singled out as a test case for TRIPs in 1996.[7] The European Union argued that Japanese copyright protection terms had cost upwards of €100 million in lost revenues for the recordings produced between 1946 and 1971. Likewise, the United States claimed damages in the realm of US$500 million. On December 26, 1996, the Japanese government capitulated and changed its copyright law to reflect its TRIPs obligations.

TRIPs has moved aspects of intellectual property protection previously in the realm of the Berne Convention and the World Intellectual Property Organization (WIPO) into WTO jurisdiction.[8] The most significant result is that large corporations are perceived by many to be in partnership with the WTO. Primary corporate objectives include market access and rules harmonization in the south and expansion of existing markets in the north. The largest transnationals, such as News Corporation of Australia and the Walt Disney Company of the United States, have been industry leaders, owning huge shares in one of the fastest-growing segments of global trade. This oligopoly is unprecedented and raises concerns among trade watchers about the future of cultural diversity (Warner, 2002).

Out of the several dozen TRIP disputes to date, seven disputes have involved cultural goods. Significantly, only two of these cases have gone all the way through the panel process. The other five cases have been classified as "mutually agreed solutions" notified under Article 3.6 of the Understanding on Rules and Procedures for the Settlement of Disputes, commonly referred to as the Dispute Settlement Understanding (DSU). In these cases, the responding countries agreed to bring their national policies into line with the TRIPs Agreement. This outcome occurred because the United States has committed significant legal resources to the defence of intellectual property. To date, only Canada and the European Union have challenged the American interpretation of intellectual property law.

United States — Section 110(5) of the US Copyright Act

The European Communities (EC) launched a music copyright case against the United States in 1999 (WTO, 1999–2001).[9] Many American retailers, restaurants, and bars freely broadcast music in their establishments. Section 110(5) of the US Copyright Act permits this, under certain conditions, without the payment of a royalty fee. The EC argued that this law contravened American obligations under the Berne Convention and the TRIPs Agreement. The music copyright case is unique in that Americans, the most vociferous of copyright protectors, were caught in a situation in which their own copyright laws were challenged and found lacking by a WTO dispute settlement panel.

Table 5.1. *Chronology of Dispute Settlement Relating to Trade in Cultural Goods*

1996

Japan—Measures Concerning Sound Recordings (DS 28/42) brought by the United States and the European Communities

Turkey—Taxation of Foreign Film Revenues (DS 43) brought by the United States

Japan—Measures Affecting Distribution Services (DS 45) brought by the United States

1997

Canada—Certain Measures Concerning Periodicals (DS 31) brought by the United States

1998

Canada—Measures Affecting Film Distribution Services (DS 117) brought by the European Communities

European Communities/Greece—Motion Pictures, TV, Enforcement (DS 124/125) brought by the United States

1999

United States—Section 110(5) of the US Copyright Act (DS 160) brought by the European Communities

Source: World Trade Organization (2009).

Gaining American compliance with this decision has been a long and arduous process. The United States was given until December 20, 2001 to comply with the panel report, but Congress has yet to comply, preferring to pay the annual €1.2 million in penalties assessed by the arbitrator. The EC continues to press the administration and Congress to bring legislation into line with TRIPs and efforts are ongoing.[10]

Canada — Certain Measures Concerning Periodicals

The first culture case to go all the way through the panel process was the American complaint against Canada's magazine regime in 1997. This was not an intellectual property case but rather a market access case. It is the most important cultural dispute to date because it is perhaps the most definitive example of a clash of cultural regulatory models at the WTO. In it, Canada defended Tariff Code 9958, a law aimed at limiting the number of split-run magazines sold in Canada. Split-run magazines are foreign titles that are republished in Canada. They include many of the most well-known American brands — *Sports Illustrated*, *Playboy*, *Cosmopolitan* — and compete for shelf space with Canadian titles. They contain advertisements primarily directed at the Canadian market, but often they directly replicate the content of the issue that was published elsewhere. Split runs are a boon for publishers because replicating their content in Canada costs virtually nothing, and advertising space can be sold over and over again. Advertisements are sold first in the home jurisdiction where the magazine is originally produced and then resold any number of times in the many different foreign markets in which the magazine is also published (Dubinsky, 1996).

In 1960, the Diefenbaker government established the O'Leary Royal Commission on Publications, which reported that 80 per cent of the magazine industry was in foreign hands. Since then, the Canadian government has made a proactive commitment to Canadian periodical publishing, using a variety of excise measures and subsidies to protect and promote the industry. In 1965, Canada enacted Tariff Code 9958, which prohibited the dumping of foreign magazines on the Canadian market. Canadian publishers view split runs as an unfair trading practice that undermines the ability of Canadian publishers to produce a made-in-Canada product. The Canadian government considers the sale of split-run magazines to be similar to the dumping of a foreign product on the Canadian market for less than the cost of production. American publishers consider split runs to be one of the efficiencies generated by economies of scale; if Canadians do not like American magazines, they do not have to buy them.

In 1995, Canada shifted its regulatory strategy to accommodate technological change by enacting Part V.I of the Excise Tax Act, which imposed a tax of 80 per cent of the value of all the advertisements inserted in split-run magazines, to be levied on each issue. At the same time, Heritage Canada began an assistance program that paid Canada Post Corporation to provide Canadian publishers with reduced postal rates that were lower than the commercial international rates applied to imported magazines. The federal Publications Assistance Program (PAP) helps defray the mailing costs for subscriptions, in recognition that the industry is facing stiffer competition for advertising dollars with split runs and online content. With the advent of digital information technology, American publishers began to evade border tariffs by publishing foreign versions of their magazines that were electronically transmitted to a Canadian printing facility. When Time Warner, the US publisher of *Sports Illustrated,* used digital technology to circumvent Tariff Code 9958, the Canadian government imposed a massive excise tax and the United States sued (Acheson & Maule, 1999).

Article III of the GATT states that a country must treat foreign products in the same way that it treats domestically produced products if they are like products, or directly competitive or substitutable products. The United States, citing market access provisions in GATT Articles III and XI, argued that Canada's magazine regime unfairly discriminated against imported products, which, in this case, were American split-run magazines. Canada responded by declaring that its magazine regime was needed to protect Canadian culture and therefore legal under GATT Article XX, the general exemption clause. This clause allows countries to exempt certain goods from the discipline of the GATT on the basis of protecting public morals, public health, and works of artistic or historic value.

Specifically, Canada defended its practice under Paragraph d, which allows countries to invoke non-discriminatory measures to ensure that other countries comply with national laws, such as customs procedures.[11] The Liberal government of Jean Chrétien regarded this to be a regulatory matter in which a standard had been set to uphold a public preference for Canadian content in domestic news magazines. This domestic imperative, the government maintained, should be reason enough for Canada to invoke the general exception clause of the GATT for the purpose of enforcing the border tax that Time Warner had evaded. Canada argued that Canadian magazines cannot be compared directly to American magazines on the basis of their physical form alone (the dispute settlement panel compared two news magazines, *Time* and *Maclean's,* in terms of size, number of pages, and type of paper used). But physical characteristics are never definitive when comparing cultural products. Canadian magazines carry content important to Canadians; their significance to maintaining Canada's cultural distinctiveness must also be considered. The important issue for Canada was whether a magazine carried uniquely Canadian cultural content.

The panel disagreed, saying that the relative distinctions for the basis of trade are physical — what kind of magazines are these? Are they similar products? If so, market share should be decided by free competition. Canada removed the import prohibition on split-run magazines through an order in council in November of 1998, and since then has supported domestic magazine publishers through a postal subsidy and an array of publishing subsidies made available through Heritage Canada.[12] In bilateral negotiations, Canada and the United States reached an agreement wherein Canadian advertisements in split-run magazines are capped at 18 per cent. Further, advertisers who buy space in magazines with no Canadian content are only able to deduct 50 per cent of their expenses on their tax returns, but those who buy space in magazines with at least 80 per cent Canadian content are able to deduct the full cost of the advertisement.[13]

TRADE REGULATION AND THE FUTURE OF TRADE IN CULTURAL GOODS

Global trade politics have added to the complexity of the issues faced by governments and cultural producers. The network of bargains in this case involved four significant categories of political actors: states, non-governmental organizations, media and entertainment corporations, and, of course, citizens. Predictably, Canada's loss at the WTO ignited a firestorm of protest from the cultural community. Activists in Canada spearheaded the formation of the International Network for Cultural Diversity that aims to influence public policy by rallying arts communities against international agreements that supposedly threaten culture. Headquartered in Toronto, the INCD has a truly international steering committee, with input provided by such leading cultural institutions as the Smithsonian in Washington, D.C., as well as by writers, artists, and cultural policy experts across North America, Europe, Africa, and Asia. The INCD coordinates its annual conferences to correspond to the annual meetings of culture ministers who form the International Network on Cultural Policy, the intergovernmental cousin of the INCD.

Following the loss at the WTO, the Canadian government realized that the tacit *exemption culturelle* that seemed to typify GATT diplomacy no longer existed.[14] The International Network on Cultural Policy is not much of an agenda setting body, but it does provide a multilateral platform from which governments may discuss relevant issues of cultural policy. It is also significant in that it rallied governmental support for a proposed instrument to protect cultural diversity. In October of 2005, Canada's two-track activist process paid dividends, when UNESCO's member states adopted the Convention on the Protection and Promotion of the Diversity of Cultural Expressions. It formally entered into force on March 18, 2007. The United States is alone in its refusal to ratify the convention.

The convention's goal is to treat cultural production and consumption as part of a single system that is unique. The UNESCO website describes culture as "five inseparable links of the same chain: creation, production, distribution/dissemination, access and enjoyment of cultural expressions."[15] At its heart is the acknowledgement that, in every cultural industry, state support has been a key factor in the growth of private production and has played a decisive role in shaping the sector. Culture may be an organic aspect of human society, like economy. But it is never directly substitutable with economic exchange.

Needless to say, the biggest winners in this dispute are multinational media and entertainment enterprises that create much of the world's most popular entertainment. These corporations have been besieged by new technology, and they had their profits eroded by the technology-savvy teenagers who used to be their most promising marketing demographic. The media giants have responded like the grumpy and out-of-touch old-timers they are, demanding tighter property rights and railing against the amorality of consumers who download *Harold & Kumar Escape from Guantanamo Bay*, rather than spending 12 dollars on a movie ticket. By controlling a product from conception through to residual licensing, the biggest media and entertainment companies have attempted to optimize returns. A summer blockbuster movie produced by Warner Bros. Studios is advertised on America Online and distributed by a Time Warner affiliate. Simultaneously, its soundtrack is released on Warner Music Group. Later, it may be licensed for cable television play on HBO and eventually make its way to a Warner-controlled network or television station. Product rolls down the pipe; licensing fees flow up (Grant & Wood, 2004).

With this business strategy, the corporate agenda for global free trade in entertainment and culture consists of three goals. The first is to build bigger national markets for cultural products. Growing the market requires convincing consumers to spend more. American consumers spend the most, accounting for at least 35 cents of every dollar spent on media and entertainment worldwide, and they are willing to spend larger portions of their wages for entertainment (PricewaterhouseCoopers, 2004). Capitalizing on this demand is of first-order importance. Concentration of ownership in the Anglo-American market is a natural outgrowth of this drive to capture the lucrative home audience. The second goal is to expand market access in underexploited jurisdictions. Using the WTO to remove public policy roadblocks to the free flow of cultural goods and services across national borders is a key to success. This aim has been difficult to achieve because national regulatory authorities often (but not always) resist a market-driven compromise on community standards. The Federal Communications Commission in the United States and the Canadian Radio-Television and Telecommunications Commission in Canada are two examples. Similar bodies are significant in Europe, China, and India. The last agenda item is to consolidate international markets with a particular focus on the global south. Expansion in the developing parts of the world is less predictable, and profits are less assured than many companies assumed when they began forays into Asia and post-communist Eastern Europe in the 1990s.

One reason that the media and entertainment titans are facing a rough ride in the developing world is that digital technology is finally in reach for those who have not had access to it in the past, including the poor, children, and the disabled. African farmers and fishermen — traditionally excluded from informed participation in the market — are using cell phones and SMS messaging to achieve higher prices for the produce they sell. Similarly, text messaging is an ideal instrument for organizing spontaneous public demonstrations in Asia's megacities. The anti-Japan demonstrations of 2005 were facilitated by text messaging, which was used to mobilize thousands of urban Chinese nationalists. Similarly, the violent Muslim demonstrations in Beirut, in which the Danish embassy was burned following the publication of anti-Muslim political cartoons in Denmark, were in part catalyzed by rumours spread via text message that Danish right-wing nationalists were going to burn the Koran.

Governments also have seen the political potential of new digital technologies, and they are increasingly sceptical of arguments that attempt to pare down complex issues to the lowest common denominator of market access. The digital revolution and the expansion of civil society it facilitates is proof positive that local and regional diversity continue to flourish in the face of corporate convergence. The resilience of domestic cultural production in an increasingly monopolistic and transnational culture industry is a big part of the global culture story and also a significant feature of Canada's booming trade in cultural goods. The question that requires more thought is, how should countries promote free trade while defending cultural pluralism? In an age of intense information flows, cultural products are an increasingly important part of every country's trade strategy. Urgent public policy issues such as the growing corporate concentration of ownership in the cultural industries, the need to safeguard language rights, and the need to bridge the digital divide for the poorest nations require governments and civil society to be innovative locally and internationally.

So far, there are no definitive answers, nor is there any consensus on how to nourish cultural diversity. Global publics are deeply divided between two visions for the future—a global culture for private economic actors or a renewed cultural pluralism for citizens. These visions are supported by two very different ways of understanding the role of WTO governance in the international economy. Transnational media and entertainment companies argue that they need a system of rules that guarantees their intellectual property rights and provides adequate enforcement mechanisms to police the global information economy. That these companies would want a strong system of patent and copyright protection is unsurprising because their business models are built around the intellectual property rules in place in North America and Europe. Deviation from these rules in the global south, or among users of new information technologies, undercuts the established business model.

The regulatory system championed by cultural pluralists and libertarian civil society activists recognizes that tighter rules for trade, including rules that treat cultural goods like any other tradeable commodity, are appropriate in some circumstances but that current trade rules cannot be applied across the board. Many in this group would like to see the enforcement of intellectual property rights take a back seat to the creation of new forms of cultural expression and to innovation in cultural transmission. They are working to improve the current trading system with an eye to promoting and strengthening cultural diversity.

CONCLUSION: THE NETWORK OF BARGAINS REVISITED

Canada's decision to pursue its vision of cultural pluralism outside the WTO represents a tacit recognition on the part of Canadian policymakers that the system may, at times, be a blunt instrument with many significant and unintended consequences. An overly vigorous approach to market access undermines the state's ability to develop an effective set of cultural policy tools. Canada continues to promote its multicultural model. The main selling feature of the Canadian regulatory model is that it protects social diversity while promoting market competition. This hybrid works for proactive national standards while emphasizing the linkages between domestic cultural producers and transnational cultural and economic actors (Zemans, 2004).

In a narrow sense, the "magazines case" influenced changes in the way that Canada subsidized magazine producers, but that is only the smallest part of the story. This case had a striking impact upon public policies in a number of different jurisdictions. It echoed far beyond Canada and was a galvanizing force behind a number of international initiatives on the part of Canadians and their federal government. Not surprisingly, the issue of cultural plural-ism has been one of the driving factors behind civil society's distrust of the WTO, both in terms of its potential homogenizing effect on world culture as well as in terms of its controversial decisions that are perceived as privileg-ing trade flows over other "non-trade" considerations. In the future, cultural issues at the WTO will be more contentious and complex because, if there is one thing that all members (including the United States) agree on, it is the central importance of culture to their economies and societies.

Notes

1. In recognition of the complex relationship between enterprise and free expres-sion in the domain of culture, every member of UNESCO signed the Convention on the Protection and Promotion of the Diversity of Cultural Expressions, except the United States and Israel. Most of the important issues dealt with in the con-vention were originally expressed in the Universal Declaration on Cultural Diversity, which was released in 2001 and enjoyed broad support among UNESCO's membership. Read the full text of the convention at http://portal.unesco. org/en/ev.php-URL_ID=31038&URL_DO=DO_TOPIC&URL_SECTION=201. htmlhttp://portal.unesco.org/en/ev.php-URL_ID=31038&URL_DO=DO_ TOPIC&URL_SECTION=201.html.

2. For the INCD's complete statement of principles, go to www.incd.net/about. html#Principles.

3. See the complete "Ministerial Statement" from the 2007 meeting of the INCP at www.incp-ripc.org/meetings/2007/index_e.shtml.

4. Max Weber's seminal study *The Protestant Ethic and the Spirit of Capitalism* is only one of many attempts to draw connections between culture and economics. Thorstein Veblen's *The Theory of the Leisure Class* and John Kenneth Galbraith's *The Affluent Society* highlight the link between economics and culture.

5. The global cultural economy is a leviathan in its complexity and market reach. According to market research by PricewaterhouseCoopers (2004), worldwide consumption of media and entertainment topped $911 billion in 2003, up 4.3 per cent from consumer spending the year before. When advertising services are also factored into the equation, the value of the global information economy is estimated at more than $1.2 trillion annually. And this number does not include the value of the services trade that often accompanies the flow of information. Not surprisingly, the growth of consumer spending on entertainment far out-stripped the growth of national economies in the 1990s, many of which expanded at a rate of 2 to 3 per cent a year. Most national governments have developed distinctive regulatory models to govern trade in cultural goods and services. The types of mechanisms used depend upon a number of factors,

including the level of development of domestic markets for culture, their relative strength vis-à-vis competitors, and the intensity of cultural flows entering national jurisdictions. Other, less obvious issues also factor into the equation, such as the importance of local language, religion, and other cultural values to domestic consumers and their governments.

6. For more analysis see Statistics Canada's *Culture Trade and Investment Project* at http://www.statcan.ca/english/freepub/87-007-XIE/culture.htm.

7. For the full text of this case, see WTO (1996) at http://www.wto.org/english/tratop_e/dispu_e/cases_e/ds28_e.htm.

8. Under the Berne Convention of 1886, countries pledged to grant the same protection to the works of other contracting states as they did to their own nationals. The TRIPs Agreement is sometimes referred to as a "Berne-plus" agreement. It goes further, in terms of raising minimum standards of protection, laying out detailed enforcement procedures, and making disputes over property rights subject to the WTO's dispute settlement rules. Never before has copyright been so staunchly defended. For more information about the history of intellectual property regulation, see www.wipo.org. See also Ivan Bernier (2000).

9. Access this case at http://www.wto.org/english/tratop_e/dispu_e/cases_e/ds160_e.htm.

10. For a summary of this ongoing dispute see the European Trade Commission's website at http://ec.europa.eu/trade/tackling-unfair-trade/dispute-settlement/.

11. The standard view of the general exceptions clause is that the laws it is invoked to protect must not be in violation of the GATT. Paragraph d has been invoked to defend environmental standards and discriminatory trade practices on the basis of conservation and public health. However, GATT Article XX was only ever successfully invoked to protect national standards in the case entitled "European Communities—Measures affecting asbestos and products containing asbestos."

12. For the text of the order in council, see Government of Canada (1998). See also on this issue Heritage Canada (2003).

13. For more information see Heritage Canada, Cultural Sector Investment Review (2003). See also Krikorian (2005, p. 958).

14. For an excellent overview of the INCD and the UNESCO Convention on the Protection and Promotion of the Diversity of Cultural Expressions, see INCD Executive Director Garry Neil's backgrounder at www.incd.net/incden.html.

15. See UNESCO's website for a backgrounder on and the full text of the Convention on the Protection and Promotion of the Diversity of Cultural Expressions: http://portal.unesco.org/culture/en/. Follow the "Cultural Diversity" links.

CHAPTER SIX

Intellectual Property Rights Enforcement: The Case of Canadian Patents

When the World Trade Organization's intellectual property rights agreement was amended in 2003 to allow members to export generic medicines to countries hard hit by HIV/AIDS, Canada was the first country to change its domestic legislation accordingly. Canada has an interest in pursuing market access for generic drug producers, and this might account for movement on the parallel importation issue. However, the Jean Chrétien Pledge to Africa Act has been used just once in four years, and non-governmental policy analysts have noted that the legislation is likely to be too cumbersome to be of much benefit to generic pharmaceutical producers.

The international trade regime is a complex institutional environment that overlaps with many other areas of public policy, and in which policy leadership has many unintended legal and political consequences. The network of bargains in this case involves two very significant groups of economic actors: patented pharmaceutical producers and generic pharmaceutical producers. This final case study examines the way that both interest groups influence the processes of international law. As a result, we will proceed with this case slightly differently in order to examine more closely how the relationship between business interests and government can have unintended consequences that nevertheless play a significant part in shaping members' foreign policy preferences.

The first section briefly examines the place of generic producers in the Canadian pharmaceutical sector. It then moves to the question of how interest group preferences shape Canadian intellectual property rights. The goal is not to provide a theory of the policy formation process or to demonstrate that a single group of interests determines public policy. Rather, the intention is to provide a suitable vantage point from which to engage with the WTO as an institutional and legal environment in which concentrated interests attempt to influence national policy strategies.

The second section focuses on the Agreement on Trade-Related Aspects of Intellectual Property Rights (TRIPs) and the contentious process that led to its provisional amendment in 2005. The global enforcement of intellectual property rights dovetails with a concerted strategy on the part of pharmaceutical companies to maintain the current corporate model of growth and profitability. The globalization of information has undermined traditional methods of protecting intellectual property and has eroded the differential pricing structure that the industry has developed over the past several decades. As a result, pharmaceutical interests have a large incentive to lobby foreign governments whose policy decisions may have an impact upon industrial strategies and corporate structure.

The final section examines two high-profile intellectual property rights cases that were brought against Canada at the WTO. Dispute settlement is one way that concentrated interests can exert pressure on national governments. The WTO acts as a regulatory frame for progressive liberalization and as an institutional mechanism for dispute settlement — and these instruments discipline the choices of member governments (Frieden & Martin, 2002). In the competitive world of trade politics, trade policies are formed within a decision matrix that includes the agendas of domestic interests, other interested parties from beyond the state, the process of liberalization negotiations, and the risks and costs associated with challenges to state law and policy in international legal venues.

Canada's losses at the WTO invalidated national legislation that had resisted the full discipline of patent protection as prescribed under TRIPs Article 28.1 and Article 33. These articles define the metaphorical heart of intellectual property protection — the basic rights of patent holders and patent term limits. Did Canada's losses have a chilling effect on Canadian policymaking vis-à-vis compulsory licensing of HIV/AIDS medications bound for Africa? Looking for a smoking gun is likely a fruitless quest. Nevertheless, these WTO panel decisions provide future policymakers with a clear indication that panels will not tolerate national strategies for social protection that infringe upon the form or substance of intellectual property rights.

In the context of intellectual property rights discipline, these cases go a significant distance in explaining Canada's risk-averse approach to crafting legislation that allows for the parallel importation of HIV medicines produced under compulsory license. In the cost-benefit logic by which governments weigh the gains from trade governance, symbolic policy leadership has fewer transaction costs when substantive policy shift is opposed by concentrated economic interests (Gattinger, 2002).

PHARMACEUTICAL INTERESTS AND CANADA'S GENERIC DRUG INDUSTRY

In all developed countries, questions of patent term length are caught up within a number of debates about corporate rights because most patent holders are corporations (Doern & Sharaput, 2000, p. 45). Canada is no exception; more than 90 per cent of all patent holders in Canada are corporations.[1] Moreover, Canada's intellectual property (IP) protection framework is fundamentally shaped by the international regulatory context because Canada has been an IP taker, rather than an IP maker, to borrow a phrase from Doern and Sharaput. As such, Canada is a relatively minor player in the creation of intellectual property protection standards. The structure of Canada's knowledge economy has always reflected the influence of innovations in the United States and Europe. As early as the 1950s, the Royal Commission on Patents, Copyright, Trade Marks, and Industrial Designs, otherwise known as the Ilsley Commission, found that more than 96 per cent of Canada's patents were granted to foreigners, and the same pattern is still seen today.

Concomitantly, branded pharmaceutical manufacturers spend very little research and development money in Canada. Measurements of research and development funding relative to population and GDP bear out this assessment. According to a 2002 report from the Patented Medicine Prices Review Board (PMPRB), both spending on research and development and on the drugs themselves is much higher in the United States and Europe. It should be noted, however, that the federal government's spending on pharmaceuticals as a share of total health care expenditure remains quite high. Pharmaceuticals account for about 16 per cent of health care spending in Canada. Only France and Italy allocate more of their health care spending for drugs — about 21 and 22 per cent respectively (PMPRB, 2004).[2]

Another ranking of knowledge economy competitiveness is the yearly patent count. Thomson Reuters ranks countries according to the number of patents filed on an annual basis. Canada ranked thirteenth globally in patent applications in 2005, with 2,193 patents applied for in that year. In comparison, the Japanese patent office recorded more than 300,000 applications, and even Australia recorded over 3,000 patent applications in the same period. The largest IP makers tend to be the traditional intellectual property powerhouses such as Japan and the United States and the emerging industrial economies, including India, Brazil, and Russia. Canada ranked ahead of most northern European countries, however. For example, Denmark reported 836 applications filed in the same 12-month period (Wild, 2006).

Focusing only on research spending levels or Canada's patent ranking obscures the larger story. Canada has a large and globally competitive generic drug industry, which accounts for at least a quarter of Canada's pharmaceutical manufacturing sector (Skinner, 2005).[3] This industry provides approximately 10,000 jobs and spends almost half a billion dollars on research and development per year, about one quarter of all pharmaceutical R & D spending in Canada. In comparison, branded drug companies spend about $1.2 billion on R & D in Canada or a little less than 1 per cent of the amount spent globally on an annual basis (PMPRB, 2004). Generic drug production has almost quadrupled in the past decade. Most generics consumed in Canada are produced here or in the United States. The generics industry has a healthy trade surplus, yet Canada's trade deficit in pharmaceuticals has grown steadily for a number of years. Most of this deficit is accounted for by the rising prices of imported, branded drugs. In dollar figures, branded drugs account for approximately 80 per cent of the Canadian drug market.

The way that economic interest informs public policy has long been a focus for scholars of international political economy. Most practitioners in the field consider the influence of organized economic interests to be an integral part of the process of policy formation. Recently, those who study the differences between European and Anglo-American "varieties of capitalism" have also begun to examine the relationship between economic interests and policymaking (Fioretos, 2001). In some of the most recent literature on European policy formation, for example, both Duer (2008) and Verdun (2008) have found that economic interests play a more prominent role in European economic integration and multilevel policy formation than has been emphasized in earlier research.

In the Canadian literature, the role of economic interests has traditionally been portrayed with a certain amount of nuance. This is at least partly because Canada has a relatively small domestic business establishment and a large contingent of branch plant manufacturers; therefore, its relationship to government is often studied sector by sector, rather than theorized in the aggregate. Canadian trade literature has been and still remains largely the study of Canada–US relations. As such, it maintains a realist understanding of trade relations as the art of the possible in which domestic interests, as variables, are dependent upon the continental political realities in which trade occurs.

The phenomenal increase in world trade over the past several decades has been a key factor in the revival of interest in the role of external constraints on public policy in the United States as well. As Milner (1997) has argued, "domestic politics and international relations are inextricably interrelated. A country's international position exerts an important impact on its internal politics and economics. Conversely, its domestic situation shapes its behaviour in foreign relations" (p. 3). In American and European literature on the role of concentrated interests in the formation of policy preferences, domestic business interests still receive the most attention. This is because domestic business interests exert a more direct influence on policymakers, and these interests are often reflected by voting constituencies. The influence of interests from outside the state is more difficult to quantify. Keohane and Milner (1996) have shown that, when international interests affect policymaking within a state, it is usually through diffuse rather than concentrated means, suggesting that, in most cases, "internationalization affects the autonomy of governments' policy choices by undermining the efficacy of some policies" rather than through more measurable means such as lobbying or public opinion campaigns (p. 15).

The politics of trade multilateralism at the WTO provides a good example of how internationalization affects domestic policy choices. The international trade regime introduces a new level of complexity because it allows for the articulation of interests beyond the domestic context through institutional means such as the dispute settlement process. In the process of crafting Canada's legislative response to the provisional amendment of TRIPs Article 31(f), legislators attempted to steer a narrow route between, on one side, the interests of Canada's generic pharmaceutical industry, those of African nations, and the demands of international civil society and, on the other side, well-organized pharmaceutical interests in the United States and Europe.

A cursory reading of the literature on interest groups would suggest that, in the Canadian context, the generics industry, which is well organized and has effectively lobbied the government in the past, would press for and receive legislation that would maximize opportunity to produce generic versions of HIV medication. However, this assumption is inadequate because it does not take into consideration the state of generic manufacturing in Canada (until 2007 no HIV/AIDS drugs were being produced), nor does it account for the significant international pressure exerted by patented pharmaceutical manufacturers. Further, it does not account for efforts of civil society actors who are pressuring national governments to amend intellectual property rules on multiple fronts, from promoting the liberal use of compulsory licensing laws (as is the practice in Thailand) to pressing for an open-source solution to the provision of AIDS medicines for Africa (Srinivas, 2006).

The Liberal government under Jean Chrétien originally introduced Bill C-56 to amend the Patent Act and the Food and Drugs Act. And the bill included a number of features that the international pharmaceutical lobby had pressed for, including a right of first refusal on contracts between developing countries and generic drug manufacturers and a restrictive list of countries eligible to import generic drugs from Canada. However, after hearing from witnesses in medical and humanitarian relief organizations and from spokespeople for generic producers and after enduring a letter-writing campaign from the National Union of Public and General Employees, the government decided to amend the bill.

Reintroduced as Bill C-9 under the Martin government, the legislation did not include a right of first refusal or a restrictive country list. It did include a list of exempt medicines that opened the possibility for companies to lobby for exemptions on a drug-by-drug basis. The bill also drew criticism for a clause that allows brand-name pharmaceutical companies to sue generic manufacturers whose deals with southern countries are suspected of being too commercial—more about profits than pandemics. Critics charge that the legislation, in its current form, allows multinational pharmaceutical firms to use litigation to bully generic producers (Chase, 2004). The final legislation appears to be a compromise between the demands of branded drug makers and a concerned coalition of doctors, NGOs, generic manufacturers, and citizens.

INTELLECTUAL PROPERTY AND PUBLIC HEALTH

Developing countries are frequently typified by small markets, distinct disease environments, and weak health care systems. Malaria, tetanus, measles, syphilis and leprosy are just a few of the diseases that are still a major burden in the global south, although they are widely eradicated in the developed world. One in four children in least developed countries do not receive the World Health Organization's Expanded Programme on Immunization, which provides tetanus, diphtheria, and pertussis inoculations—shots that cost only pennies a child and require hardly any expertise and infrastructure to administer (Kremer, 2002, p. 69). Sales of medicine on the continent of Africa account for just 1 per cent of the market for branded pharmaceuticals. Whereas combined public and private health care spending on pharmaceuticals recently topped $4,000 per person in the United States, health care providers in Africa spent an average of $18 per capita.[4] Research and development spending patterns reflect this fact. Of the 1,200 drugs licensed worldwide between 1975 and 1997, only 13 were intended for the treatment of tropical diseases. And 5 of these were derived from veterinary research.

Over the past several decades, the United States and some members of the European Union have faced increasing competition from firms in developing countries that imitate the innovative products and techniques developed by countries in the global north. Throughout the 1980s, intellectual property rights rose on the international trade agenda until they were finally formally included in the Final Act Embodying the Results of the Uruguay

Round and the North American Free Trade Agreement. Of specific concern were the shorter periods of patent protection offered in some jurisdictions and the trade in pirated goods, from counterfeit handbags to sound recordings shared over the Internet. In trade theory, there is a simple and compelling reason to protect rather than liberalize the trade in patented goods and services: "unless invention or creation is compensated at its full social value, there will be sub-optimal incentives to undertake it" (Trebilcock & Howse, 1999, p. 309).

The basic goal of TRIPs is to ensure that inventors receive a uniform level of protection across member jurisdictions. Before the Agreement on Trade-Related Aspects of Intellectual Property Rights came into force in 1995, these rights were minimally regulated at the international level, and there were no integrated international enforcement measures to ensure standards. The World Intellectual Property Organization (WIPO) provided a forum for the harmonization of IP rights between signatory countries, but policing enforcement was largely a national issue.

The Office of the United States Trade Representative (USTR) began the trend of linking IP rights to international trade when, having grown frustrated with piracy and lack of security for American industrial patents, it began to enforce American patents unilaterally in the US Court of International Trade under Special 301 provisions. The TRIPs Agreement, although deeply unpopular in the global south, promised an end to unilateral American action on the patent front, and WTO dispute settlement was considered a better prospect than defending government action, or lack thereof, in an American court. TRIPs harmonizes IP treatment and creates standards for enforcement, although IP protection remains rooted in domestic law (Heiskanen, 2004). Patents must be protected for a term of 20 years; before this, every member of WIPO set independent patent term limits.[5]

The globalization of intellectual property has placed the dominant business model, in which firms develop and patent products and processes and then sell them at whatever price national markets will bear, under increasing strain. In many of the countries where demand for life-saving medicines is highest, there is little ability to pay for product and very few safeguards in place to protect intellectual property. Further, generic firms in these areas have been quick to reverse-engineer patented products and sell them in the grey markets for medicines that flourish in impoverished parts of the world (Glassman, 2005).

TRIPs is essential to the two-pronged strategy currently pursued by the transnational pharmaceutical sector in order to shore up its troubled corporate model. The largest actors are building vertically integrated drug empires to protect profits in an era of global uncertainty. Mergers and acquisitions are the preferred way to capitalize upon the economies of scale made possible by the TRIPs Agreement. The vertical integration of brand-name pharmaceutical firms with generic manufacturers and suppliers is the dominant business model in the sector today because this model allows parent companies to generate larger profits from patent rents.[6] This approach involves the use of product life cycle extension strategies, in which patents are renewed after changing drug formulas. Industry leaders are also aggressively combating all patent challenges through the WTO's comprehensive IP protection regime. Maintaining a dominant position through patents and vertical integration is the industry's best hope for riding out the tsunami of generic production and unregulated consumption that typifies the grey market for medicines in a large number of the WTO's poorest members.

In 2000, more than 20 of the world's largest pharmaceutical patent holders threatened to sue South Africa over its decision to allow compulsory licenses for HIV treatment drugs. South Africa has one of the highest AIDS infection rates in the world, and, at the time, antiretroviral treatments cost upwards of $10,000 per person, per year. Following the public outcry over the misuse of pharmaceutical patents, the case was dropped. Yet it became one of the catalysts behind patent reform at the WTO (Park, 2002). When, in response to the anthrax scare in the United States in 2000 and 2001, the American government threatened to use compulsory licensing to manufacture an antidote, in effect following South Africa's lead when public health was threatened, the hypocrisy of the hardline position on patent protection was revealed. The South African public relations debacle in 2000 and the 2001 over the anthrax scare in the United States, at which time the American government threatened to use compulsory licensing to manufacture an antidote, showed the hypocrisy of the hardline position on patent protection (Mercurio, 2004, p. 222).[7] The launch of the Doha Round in 2001 was the first time that international public health and development issues were discussed at all levels of the WTO.

The Doha Ministerial Declaration, issued at the end of the trade talks in Qatar, only dealt with the issue of compulsory licenses, leaving out the more contentious issue of parallel importing, which was only resolved through a WTO waiver in 2003. The waiver temporarily amended TRIPs Article 31(f) to allow countries with drug manufacturing capabilities to manufacture medicines under compulsory licenses in order to export them to countries without manufacturing sectors. The WTO called on members to amend their national laws accordingly and assured them that countries exporting drugs under this new regime would not face litigation.[8]

The amendment, which marks the first time a WTO agreement has been changed, was incorporated into TRIPs at the end of 2005.[9] In the original text, TRIPs Article 27 and 31 allow compulsory licensing of patented drugs, but only if the generic medicines produced are for domestic use and the compulsory license does not unreasonably infringe upon the patent rights conferred in Article 28.[10] The amendment stipulates that importing countries must have no domestic manufacturing ability, and exporting countries must inform the WTO of intent to manufacture and export medicines on a country-by-country, drug-by-drug basis.[11] The African group of member countries reluctantly supported the amendment, but the group maintained its claim that the conditions of the waiver do not take into account the reality that an economy of scale is required to attract the interests of major producers; selling one drug to one country through a slow and bureaucratic process might prove to be a disincentive to provide drugs to least developed countries.

Amending TRIPs Article 31(f) was no small feat of multilateral cooperation considering the opposition the measure faced. In 2001, the United States was the only country to veto the declaration of the United Nations Commission on Human Rights that defined access to HIV treatment as a fundamental human right (Park, 2002, p. 151). Even up to the early months of 2003, the United States was the lone holdout in implementing the December 16, 2002 draft of the Doha Declaration, which called for better access to essential medicines for the poorest countries (Mercurio, 2004, p. 228). The biggest reason behind US resistance to the draft was that large pharmaceutical manufacturers had opposed the waiver on the grounds that it could be misused to divert global flows of cheap generic drugs — an undesirable scenario to an industry in which profits depend upon differential pricing schemes across many national markets.

CANADA'S INTELLECTUAL PROPERTY RIGHTS PANELS AT THE WTO

Two cases have been particularly instructive of how IP issues that relate to public health have been treated in dispute settlement at the WTO. These cases also offer insight into why Canada's policy on generic exports has adhered so closely to the ambivalent track laid by the 2003 waiver and the subsequent amendment of TRIPs Article 31(f). In 1997, the European Union sued Canada over its Patent Act, which allowed generic drug manufacturers to reverse-engineer patented drugs and then manufacture and stockpile generic supplies before the expiration of the original patent in order to allow generic manufacturers to get their product to market as soon as possible.

The case "Canada–Patent Protection of Pharmaceutical Products" concerned two aspects of Canada's Patent Act that granted exemptions to the rights of patent holders. Section 55.2(1) allows for the construction, use, or

sale of patented inventions for the "development and submission of information required under any law of Canada, a province, or a country other
than Canada that regulates the manufacture, construction, use or sale of any
product." This regulatory review provision allows the reverse engineering of
patented products in preparation for commercial competition after the
expiry of intellectual property protection. Section 55.2(2), the second exception, allowed "for the manufacture and storage of articles intended for the
sale after the date on which the term of the patent expires." The so-called
stockpiling provision allowed generic producers to manufacture generic
copies of drugs six months prior to the expiry of the patent.

The European Communities argued that both of these provisions violated TRIPs Article 28.1, which confers exclusive rights to the patent holder
"where the subject matter of a patent is a product, to prevent third parties
not having the owner's consent from the acts of making, using, offering for
sale, selling, or importing for these purposes that product." Canada agreed
that the regulatory review provision and the stockpiling provision were
exceptions to the intellectual property rights protection guaranteed under
TRIPs Article 28.1, but Canada argued that these were legal under TRIPs
Article 30, the general exceptions clause.

The panel began by examining the stockpiling provision and found that
it was not justified under Article 30 and therefore violated Article 28.1. Article 28.1 lays out five legal rights that stem from a patent: making, using,
offering for sale, selling, and importing. Stockpiling infringes these rights
and cannot be justified under Article 30. Article 30 lays out three criteria
upon which exceptions to the rights of the patent holder may be made.
Exceptions must be limited, they must not conflict with the normal exploitation
of a patent, and they must not unreasonably prejudice the interests of the
patent owner. "Members may provide limited exceptions to the exclusive
rights conferred by a patent, provided that such exceptions do not unreasonably conflict with the normal exploitation of the patent and do not
unreasonably prejudice the legitimate interests of the patent owner, taking
account of the legitimate interests of third parties."

Canada argued that Article 7, which states that intellectual property
rights should contribute to the promotion of technological innovation, and
Article 8, which allows members to "adopt measures necessary to protect
health and nutrition," should be read together as a "call for a liberal interpretation of the three conditions stated in Article 30 of the Agreement"
(WTO, 2000, para. 7.24). Canada was concerned about protecting the flexibility of Article 30 as it relates to legitimate interests of third parties. The
panel decided that the first criterion of Article 30, that the exception must be
limited, was not met by the stockpiling provision. Canada's legislation did

not place limits on the quantities of product stockpiled and further infringed upon patent rights by allowing stockpiling for up to six months.

In examining the regulatory review provision in Canada's Patent Act, the panel considered that the issue was again whether the provision could be justified under the three criteria set out in Article 30. The panel found that the regulatory review provision met the standard for an exception under Article 30 because it was a limited exception that did not unreasonably conflict with the normal exploitation of the patent and did not unreasonably prejudice the legitimate interests of the patent owner. The panel noted that the issue of regulatory review provisions was well known at the time that TRIPs was negotiated and that it was not mentioned in the text of the agreement. Therefore, rather than extend the concept of "legitimate interests" to decide the appropriateness of regulatory review provisions, it should leave the issue to be resolved through political means in the future (para 7.82).

Public health advocates have argued that the time required to bring generic medicines to market amounts to a de facto patent extension, during which time patent holders continue to enjoy a monopoly market position. Drache and Singh note that this decision, on the surface, appears to be a victory for public health because it facilitates the manufacture of generic drugs. However, by striking down the stockpiling measure, the panel continued a tradition at dispute settlement of splitting the difference when ruling on complex regulatory cases in which competing national interpretations of the agreement in question have influenced divergent regulatory regimes (Picciotto, 2003). The panel tended to favour a narrow definition of WTO legal principles, one that preserves the rights of trading partners at the expense of broader legal thinking.

Abbott (2003) disagrees, noting that, in the absence of agreement between Canada and the EC about the composition of the panel, Director-General Renato Ruggiero appointed Robert Hudec, one of the foremost scholarly authorities on international trade law in the world. Professor Hudec and the other two panellists — one of whom was a Hungarian expert in copyright law and the other the director of Mexico's National Institute of Public Health — were aware that, due to the political sensitivity of public health issues at the WTO, their decision was likely to be scrutinized for years to come. He argues that approval of Canada's regulatory review provision was a major step towards protecting the interests of public health and that striking down the stockpiling provision was inevitable because it did not stipulate any production constraints. Of the two provisions, the former was of significant importance for the future of public health provision because it protects policy space for reverse engineering, the latter mainly inconvenienced Canada's generic drug manufacturers. This decision against stockpiling is also of significance, however, because it highlights the rising value of generic production in the global marketplace for medicines.

In the case "Canada–Term of Patent Protection," the United States challenged the length of patent terms provided by Canada's Patent Act. In the act, patent term limits were determined by whether a patent was issued before or after October 1, 1989, the date on which the Patent Act was amended to provide full patent protection. Section 44 of the act limits terms on patents issued after October 1, 1989 to 20 years. Section 45 covers patents that were issued before that date, sometimes referred to as "Old Act" patents. These patents were granted a statutory protection term of 17 years (WTO, 2000a, para. 2.2).

The TRIPs Agreement requires that countries protect patents for a minimum term of 20 years. The United States argued that the patent term limit set under section 45 was inconsistent with Canada's obligations under TRIPs Article 33 and 70. Article 33 reads, "the term of protection available shall not end before the expiration of a period of twenty years counted from the filing date." The American case covered patents granted prior to October 1, 1989 and which would not expire prior to January 1, 1996, the date when TRIPs came into effect for Canada.

The Canadian Intellectual Property Office, estimated that more than 230,000 "Old Act" patents were in effect in 2000, when the panel submitted its final report. Of these, at least 140,000 would not expire until after the 20-year period. However, at least 90,000 patents, about 49 per cent of all "Old Act" patents, would not receive a full 20 years of patent protection. For most of these, however, the patent would expire sometime in the latter portion of the nineteenth year of coverage. The United States did not contest this document, but, nevertheless, it requested an expedited consideration of the dispute on the basis that its industries were suffering "irreparable harm" (WTO, 2000a, para. 1.5). Ultimately, scheduling conflicts prevented the case from being fast-tracked.

The United States argued that, pursuant to TRIPs Article 70.2, Old Act patents ought to be subject to the 20-year patent term stipulated in Article 33. Article 70.2 states, "Except as otherwise provided for in this Agreement, this Agreement gives rise to obligations in respect of all *subject matter existing at the date of application of this Agreement for the Member in question*, and which is protected in that Member on the said date, or which meets or comes subsequently to meet the criteria for protection under the terms of this Agreement" (emphasis added). Canada replied that Article 70.1, which states that the agreement "does not give rise to obligations *in respect of acts which occurred before the date of application of the Agreement* for the Member in question," exempted Old Act patents because they were granted through "acts" that occurred prior to January 1, 1996 (emphasis added).

Through textual analysis the panel found that the term "acts" in Article 70.1 and "subject matter" in Article 70.2 cover different concepts. Further, the requirement in Article 70.1 that obligations under TRIPs do not apply to discrete acts that occurred prior to January 1, 1996 does not conflict with the requirement of Article 70.2 that imposes these obligations on all existing subject matter. The basis for this argument is the public law principle that assumes all treaty provisions to be in basic harmony with the intentions of the entire agreement and thereby discourages tribunals from finding contradictions among the different provisions of a single treaty. The panel's reasoning seems to suggest that the "acts" referred to in Article 70.1 are property protections not specified by TRIPs or patents shorter than 20 years but that expired before the application of the agreement to the member in question. In short, the panel denied Canada the loophole sought in Article 70.1.

The panel rejected Canada's argument and maintained that patent holders are entitled to comprehensive protection and that TRIPs "does not state or imply that certain rights or obligations can be detached and considered in isolation" (WTO, 2000a, para. 6.54). It also rejected Canada's argument that, although its patent regime had formal provisions for 17 years of protection, it was equivalent protection because statutory and informal waiting periods around the processing of patent applications made the protection period a de facto 20-year period. The panel found that equivalent protection was not equal to statutory protection. Because Canada's Patent Act did not make available a minimum term of 20 years for patent protection, as mandated by TRIPs Article 33, Canada must bring its legislation into line with the agreement. The case was appealed and the Appellate Body upheld the panel decision on all points. With this case, the Office of the United States Trade Representative showed itself committed to upholding and promoting TRIPs as a minimum standard of acceptable protection.

CONCLUSION: THE NETWORK OF BARGAINS

There is no direct evidence that these cases influenced Canadian public policy in the wake of the TRIPs amendment. Nevertheless, the relationship between the domestic and international actors adds to a complex decision matrix in which the impact of these panels should not be underemphasized. A number of other possible causative factors (such as the political pressures mentioned earlier) no doubt contributed to the final shape of the legislation. At the domestic level, economic and industrial factors have contributed to the lacklustre performance of the new legislation. Drug prices have fallen significantly, largely due to inexpensive Indian generic products. Of equal importance is the fact that Canadian generics producers do not regularly manufacture patented HIV drugs, and Indian manufacturers do. Furthermore, compulsory licenses for parallel importation under the new agreement are only valid for two years. Obtaining a license, manufacturing, and testing may take a year or more. Canadian companies are hard pressed to recoup their costs in the limited period specified in TRIPs (Canadian Generic Pharmaceutical Association, 2004). Recently, Apotex Inc. has secured a license to manufacture 15.6 million tablets of Apo-TriAvir, a combination of three patented medicines (WTO, Council for Trade-Related Aspects of International Property Rights, 2007). The medicine will be sold to Rwanda at cost (Apotex received final tender approval from the Rwandan government in the spring of 2008), thereby neutralizing the potential of lawsuits from patent holders. Under the current rules of the Canadian Access to Medicines Regime (CAMR), licenses can only be issued for one product exported to one country. There is no provision for an open-source solution to the access problems facing African HIV/AIDS patients at this time.

At the international level, ideational and institutional factors also need to be considered in order to understand Canada's seemingly reluctant movement on this issue. The WTO's mechanisms for dispute settlement and liberalization negotiation are costly, time consuming, and knowledge intensive. These factors contribute to the massive institutional investment that members need to make in order to use the system to best advantage. With respect to the issue of generic drugs for Africa, Canada's policymakers steered a narrow course between the liberalization appeals of generic producers and the demands of foreign patent holders.

Amongst trade scholars, it is frequently asserted that the removal of obvious barriers to trade, such as tariffs, uncovers the less obvious barriers, such as subsidies. Hudec (1999a) refers to these non-tariff barriers as stumps submerged in a swamp. As high tariffs come down, the stumps begin to show above the waterline. To extend the metaphor, Canada's policy response recognizes that the removal of one barrier to humanitarian intervention will uncover other factors that complicate policy leadership. Trade litigation is one of the biggest risks associated with leadership on the parallel importation issue. Canada's risk-averse approach to crafting and implementing domestic legislation underscores this singularly important factor.

TRIPs reflects the basic interests of innovating firms and is essential to the strategy by which American and European drug manufacturers are dealing with the negative externalities of international markets, such as a downward pressure on drug prices and an increasing international trade in grey-market and black-market pharmaceuticals. The amendment of the TRIPs Agreement in 2005 marked the first time that a core WTO agreement has been altered, and the amendment represents a significant achievement for public health advocates and interested states. This makes Canada's cautious response to the amendment of TRIPs Article 31(f) somewhat surprising from the perspective of national interest and suggests that, in this case, international factors played a role in determining policy preferences.

In the case of the Jean Chrétien Pledge to Africa Act, it appears as though Canadian policymakers have developed trade-friendly international health policies that give only symbolic support to the looming needs of the WTO's poorest members. Symbolic leadership costs less than a substantive policy shift, especially in an institution in which concentrated economic interests have recourse to a binding process of dispute settlement. On one level, Canada's policy response reflects the disapproval of the United States and the scepticism of the European Union towards the parallel importation of patented medicines. But, on another level, perhaps there is simply not enough at stake for policymakers and Canadian producers to seriously test the new TRIPs flexibilities.

Notes

1. The past century has seen a steady increase in the number of patents held by corporations. In 1908, 97 per cent of Canadian patents went to individual inventors. By the 1960s, about two-thirds of patents were going to corporations, with individuals holding the remaining portion. In the intervening 40 years, the trend has continued. In 2003–2004, the top ten patentees, all multinational corporations, accounted for 1,031 patents, an average of more than 100 patents per company. See CIPO (2004).

2. This comparison was carried out because Canada's price controls and its practice of buying drugs in bulk had been criticized by branded manufacturers, who argued that their inability to recoup research and development costs in the Canadian market might prompt them to divest themselves of Canadian holdings; this threat was made during the height of the controversy over American consumers buying drugs from Canadian online pharmacies and undertaking cross-border drug-buying excursions between 2004 and 2006.

3. In 1994, Canadians consumed 3.4 times more generics than were exported by the Canadian pharmaceutical sector in the same period. In 2003, they consumed 2.6 times as many as were shipped to other countries. The trade gap shrank slightly, but the big story is that demand for generics grew by a factor of four. Higher prices at the pharmacy counter are the result of Canada's reliance on drug

imports. A recent Fraser Institute study found that branded drugs are a little cheaper in Canada than in the United States, but generics are sometimes more expensive here than in other countries.

4. The United States accounts for approximately 40 per cent of the world market for pharmaceuticals; Europe accounts for 26 per cent; Japan for 15 per cent; Latin America, Southeast Asia, and China for 15 per cent; Canada for 2 per cent, the Middle East for 1 per cent; and Africa for 1 per cent.

5. The World Intellectual Property Organization manages the Collection of Laws for Electronic Access (CLEA) database, which provides electronic copies of intellectual property legislation from over 100 countries. It can be accessed at www.wipo.int/clea/en/index.jsp.

6. Pharmaceutical research and development is characterized by very high fixed costs and relatively low marginal costs of production. A company requires large profits from successful drugs to pay for new research. Patents, not first-mover advantages, provide protection for innovators. For pharmaceutical companies, profits are guaranteed wherever patent regulations are in place and enforced by governments. Consequently, pharmaceutical regulation and prescription requirements facilitate a level of price discrimination between national jurisdictions not seen in other industries.

7. At present, approximately 40 million people have HIV, a group larger than the entire population of Canada. More than 23 million people have died of AIDS as of December 2005. In any given year, about 3 million people will succumb to AIDS, and 5 million more will be infected with HIV. By comparison, the influenza pandemic of 1918 killed between 20 and 40 million people. In Africa, the epidemic has entered the general population, whereas, in most other regions of the world, it remains contained in high-risk populations. Seventy per cent of all AIDS deaths to date have occurred in sub-Saharan Africa, where, on average, 7.5 per cent of the continent is HIV positive. For the countries hardest hit, such as Botswana and Swaziland, prevalence rates soar above 35 per cent. By comparison, the North American and European prevalence rates remain below 1 per cent of the population.

8. Parameters for the use of this mechanism are laid out in a complex seven-paragraph annex to TRIPs, which covers terms of use and protects participants in this regime from panel complaints. At the same time, the WTO also gave least developed countries (LDCs) until 2016 to extend patent protection to all medicines; the previous deadline had been 2006.

9. Technically, the amendment still had the force of a waiver in 2005 because the appropriate number of members had yet to ratify the amendment. Ninety-nine member signatures were needed by 2007 in order for the amendment to be per-

manently adopted. See the WTO's dedicated web page for notifications regarding the use of this amendment: http://www.wto.org/english/tratop_e/trips_e/public_health_e.htm.

10. The text of TRIPs Article 28 reads:

> "1. A patent shall confer on its owner the following exclusive rights:
> (a) where the subject matter of a patent is a product, to prevent third parties not having the owner's consent from the acts of: making, using, offering for sale, selling, or importing for these purposes that product;
> (b) where the subject matter of a patent is a process, to prevent third parties not having the owner's consent from the act of using the process, and from the acts of: using, offering for sale, selling, or importing for these purposes at least the product obtained directly by that process.
> 2. Patent owners shall also have the right to assign, or transfer by succession, the patent and to conclude licensing contracts."

11. In order to placate nervous pharmaceutical manufacturers, the chairperson of the WTO General Council recorded a key shared understanding of members, stating that the waiver would only be used to protect public health and providing that any member who could bring any matter of interpretation or implementation of the waiver directly to the TRIPs council for expeditious review.

CHAPTER SEVEN

Trade Litigation and the Future of Public Policy

"... we need to remember that trade is only a tool to elevate the human condition; the ultimate impact of our rules on human beings should always be at the centre of our consideration. We should work first for human beings and for the well-being of our humanity."

— WTO Director-General Pascal Lamy Santiago, Chile
January 30, 2006

Canada's network of bargains around trade litigation can be analysed in two different dimensions: first, in terms of Canada's place in the structure of the global economy and, second, in terms of the country's place in a rules-driven system. Only by examining both power and law can we begin to see the significant issues that face policymakers. In this final chapter, I will review the lessons of Canada's experience. How should we assess the overall impact of these cases on Canadian public policy? What do these cases tell us about Canadian litigation strategies, and what is their significance for the successful use of the WTO's dispute settlement mechanism in the future? These are big questions that will occupy scholars and policymakers in the future, and I do not pretend to have definitive answers. But I will venture to say that Canada must take a principled stance in its use of dispute settlement, one that examines the nation's interests in the context of the big picture of Canadian foreign policy. Trade cannot be divorced from humanitarianism, nor can Canadians afford to accept anything less than Canada's full share in the global trading system. Policymakers must walk a fine line— never sacrificing Canadians' democratic and civic values on the altar of national interest but also never losing sight of the power dynamics that decide international relations.

The WTO has been a powerful force for the development of international trade law, and its influence on domestic politics is only beginning to be understood. However, these cases suggest that the WTO has less direct influence on policy than do domestic groups. Its influence is felt in more subtle ways. As an institution, it is certainly a game changer. And perhaps its reshaping of the trading system places it front and centre in much trade policy analysis. How then should Canadian policymakers respond to the institutionalization of rules that may conflict with the way that Canadians have conducted business in the past? How should they respond to a trading system in which large questions of equity and fairness have risen in importance? These normative questions need to be addressed because the world's trading system is changing. Not only is the WTO an institution in flux but also the global financial crisis and the rise of China have added complicating dimensions to the problem of global economic leadership.

The final section turns to the issue of system evolution. The Doha Round of trade negotiations has run out of gas, and the global financial crisis has shaken confidence in American economic leadership. The Unites States will remain at the centre of the global economic system for the foreseeable future, but nobody believes any longer that the American model of capitalism is necessarily better than its competitors. How should Canada construct its trading relationships in order to benefit from both the lessons learned in dispute settlement and the changing context of global trade? Successful nations will be those who walk the walk as well as they talk the talk. Canada must live up to its humanitarian values in the way it organizes its trade relations. It is no longer possible for trading nations to treat global trade as if it were a hermetically sealed policy space that does not overlap with other social, political, and humanitarian considerations. Canada's long-term trade strategy would be best served by a development-focused policy that defines Canada's membership at the WTO in terms of both Canadian humanitarian values and trading interests.

POWER, LAW, AND THE NETWORK OF BARGAINS

Canada's network of bargains has two distinct elements: the structural features of the international economy that give it context and the rules-based system of the WTO that gives it form and content. Power is a significant and elusive variable — we know where its influence is felt, but it is difficult, or perhaps impossible, to measure quantitatively the role of power in international affairs. Susan Strange (2003) reminds us that there are two forms of power. Relational power is the power to influence other actors. Nye (2004) has described this type of power as the power to get a person (or a nation) to do what you want them to do. It may take the form of coercion, or it may have a softer shape, such as getting people to do what you want them to do by attracting them with the power of ideas.

In contrast, structural power is the power to set the rules of the game. Structural power is the result of a preponderance of relational power. A nation with a vast capacity for relational power may find that its interests routinely triumph in international politics because its power resources (be they military power, market power, or the power of ideas) are greater than those of any other single partner or rival. Such was the case with Britain at the height of its empire, and such has been the case with the United States since World War II. Structural power influences outcomes behind the scenes. It is not directly coercive or attractive. It arranges variables so that the benefits that accrue to the hegemon are a foregone conclusion.

As a result, structural power is often discussed in terms of justice. Social justice may be defined as the distribution of equitable outcomes to those nations and individuals who do not possess much structural power. In these case studies, I have focussed less on the question of whether inequality among nations is fundamentally just and more on the fact of inequality itself as it relates to policy strategy. We must admit its significance in the Canada–US relationship, but I have not attempted to determine whether Canada has gotten a raw deal because of its place in the world economy. In certain places, I have questioned the strategy of policymakers, but, as far as I am concerned, inequality is one of the defining elements of the international system. This is not to argue that Canadians ought to be content with the current state of trade and industrial policy. Rather, it is to say that structural power is a result of a number of factors including natural endowments, demographics, technological and financial capacity, and even political will. Some of these factors can be exploited in a way that increases a nation's power or moderates the power of others. Other factors cannot be changed, and vulnerability must be factored into the final equation.

In the WTO system, law was supposed to remove power, to a certain extent, as the deciding factor in trade disputes. But we have seen that, in any system predicated upon state sovereignty, power is always a significant variable. Power has a way of working its way into the system, whether it is in the way that big traders strong-arm small traders in liberalization negotiations or in the way that bilateral dispute negotiation seems to favour the more powerful country. In theoretical terms, much has been made of the power imbalance between Canada and the United States. Canada is a mouse in bed with an elephant, to use Trudeau's evocative turn of phrase. But, in practical terms, this observation means little beyond what we already know. In fact, it seems that dispute settlement has been an adequate forum for addressing trade irritants, if you factor into the equation Canada's structural disadvantages vis-à-vis the United States. Nevertheless, there are a number of lessons to be learned from the cases presented in this book. Following are the top five lessons that scholars and policymakers should take away from Canada's disputes at the WTO.

LESSON ONE: Dispute settlement does not always resolve frictions in Canada–US trade because powerful political interests are behind the predatory use of contingent protection measures. In the softwood cases, American timber producers charged that Canada's provincially-run forest management programs are against WTO subsidy rules, but what they were really concerned about is that Canada's comparative advantage in lumber comes, in part, from a very different regulatory model than the one used in the United States. On April 27, 2006, Canada and the United States agreed to a deal for the embattled timber sector. The United States agreed to lift the 10 per cent countervailing duty on softwood imports and to refund 80 per cent of the 5 billion dollars collected in duties. Canada agreed to cap its market share at 34 per cent by collecting a sliding tax, which rises as the price of lumber in the United States falls below US$355 per thousand board feet.[1] This deal is in place until 2013, with an option to renew for two more years.

This is the third time Canada has imposed quantitative restrictions on its lumber industry. There are few substantive differences between this deal and the Softwood Lumber Agreement (SLA) negotiated in 1996. The combination of export charges and volume restraints in this deal is remarkably similar to the fees charged for exceeding quantitative limits set out in the SLA. It seems incredible that Canada would walk away from litigation when it was winning. Governments play the hands they are dealt; but, in this case, Canada had a royal flush and folded in order to make a side deal. Embarrassingly, the US Court of International Trade ruled in October of 2006 that Canada was entitled to the return of all duties collected — two months after Canada cut a deal that some timber insiders refer to as the "softwood sell-out agreement" (Gibson, 2006). In this set of circumstances, Canada might have used the momentum from its multiple wins at the NAFTA Secretariat and the WTO to see the dispute all the way through all legal channels before agreeing to a settlement.

Certainly, ten wins reinforce the basic legality of the Canadian regulatory model in the context of WTO law. But the issue is not so clear-cut — especially now that Canada has abandoned its litigation option. The panels allowed that stumpage fees are actionable under the Agreement on Subsidies and Countervailing Measures, but disagreed with US methods for determining duties. This means that stumpage fees are not illegal under WTO law, yet they can be challenged in the future by any member who can make a case against Canada's framework for regulating softwood lumber harvesting. Even though a deal has been reached in this round of the lumber dispute, there is nothing in US law or WTO law that would prevent future challenges to Canada's system of stumpage fees. And certainly the fact that the Government of Canada strong-armed the industry into dropping all lawsuits and accepting the deal could well mean more legal challenges in the future.

LESSON TWO: WTO panels are reluctant to develop case law that advocates a single regulatory model for industry, and this is a good thing for Canada, even though it may not bode well for future American trade challenges. As I showed in the softwood and wheat cases, WTO panels have attempted to step lightly in order to avoid entanglement in a debate over regulatory approaches. Overall, panels in these cases developed a measured and responsible approach to the application of international law. The American case against the Canadian Wheat Board attacked the overall regulatory model by which it oversees the sale of western Canadian wheat. It also raised the issue of the unfair treatment of American wheat in the Canadian transportation system and storage facilities.

In political terms, the case was part of a larger attack on government intervention in an industry in which Canadian producers compete directly with American producers. The divergent trajectories of Canadian and American commercial regulation are starkly seen in this case. In order to illustrate American attitudes towards state trading, Annand (2000) compares the GATT's and the US Government Accountability Office's definition of state trading enterprises (STEs). The Uruguay Round Understanding on the Interpretation of Article XVII of GATT 1994 defines STEs as "Governmental and nongovernmental enterprises, including marketing boards, which have been granted exclusive or special rights or privileges, including statutory or constitutional powers, in the exercise of which they influence through their purchases or sales the level or direction of imports or exports." A 1996 Government Accountability Office (GAO) report defines STEs as "enterprises that are authorized to engage in trade and are owned, sanctioned, or otherwise supported by the government" (US GAO, 1996). The key difference is that the GATT definition focuses on the impact of STEs on trade while the GAO definition focuses on their relationship to government, that is, the fact that they are not private actors.

This definitional difference goes to the heart of the unfair trade complaint. In the American institutional context, STEs are perceived to engage in unfair trade because they are at least marginally dependent upon their governments as the source of monopoly rights and therefore not always subject to the discipline of the market. Their buying and selling may be guided by factors other than market discipline. Of course, it is not only an American view. The Conservative Party of Alberta and the federal Conservative Party (not to mention a significant portion of western farmers) also share that view and favour the dismantling of the Canadian Wheat Board.

The WTO found that there is nothing wrong with government operating a state trading enterprise that markets domestic produce abroad. The implicit argument of the American case was that the Wheat Board aimed to sell as much Canadian wheat as possible, regardless of price, in order to aid western farmers. This would drive up the Canadian supply of wheat, even if there were less demand for it on the world market, distorting international trade and driving down the international price of wheat. It is doubtful that the Canadian Wheat Board, with its small market share, would have been able to influence the price of wheat singlehandedly. I suspect that this argument is based purely on the speculation of analysts who were likely in the pay of farmers and marketers that compete with the Wheat Board. That is not to say that their case was not based upon up-to-date economic theory. Rather, it is to suggest that the impact of the Wheat Board on wheat demand is more theoretical than real.

There remains a good economic argument for using a state trading enterprise to sell wheat. The prices of agricultural goods fluctuate (sometimes wildly) from year to year. Price fluctuation can be caused by increased demand on the part of importing countries, increases and decreases in supply, weather conditions, war, economic uncertainty, and a host of other factors. The panel report seems to suggest that American litigators bit off more than they could chew when they attempted to make a case against the concept of a wheat board itself, rather than attacking certain of the Canadian Wheat Board's practices and policies. In fact, when the case was limited to aspects of Canadian regulation, it succeeded.

LESSON THREE: WTO dispute settlement is now part of the arsenal of competitive weapons employed by states in an increasingly crowded international marketplace. It was inevitable that dispute settlement would find its way into the competitive strategies of large multinational corporations and the states that support them. Just as litigation at the national level has many uses, so does dispute settlement, it seems. Especially in the civil aircraft industry, dispute settlement has been a successful strategy for challenging the public financing of competitors. Commercial banks and private investors are often unable and unwilling to sustain the risk associated with aerospace research, development, and purchase financing. It may take a decade or more for investments to pay dividends because of the time needed to develop, test, and sell a new model of aircraft. Aerospace producers and their national governments recognize this. The WTO also tacitly recognizes it. The rulings in the Bombardier and Embraer cases do not find that government funding is never required, only that it must be provided at market rates and through mechanisms that do not convey a material benefit linked to export performance. These rulings establish the fine line between legal and illegal subsidies.

All things considered, these panel decisions were somewhat progressive and might have been a bigger regulatory victory for the WTO than they actually were, had they not been blunted by blatant non-compliance. Canada and Brazil continue to subsidize their aircraft industries heavily, and both use preferential financing programs to sell airplanes. It seems that both suits were aimed at consolidating market gains and undermining competitors and had little to do with a sincere belief that government intervention conveyed an unfair advantage. A further lesson is that, if panel reports go against the grain of national interest, some members will evade WTO discipline even as they continue to use dispute settlement as a continuation of trade policy by other means. In fact, this same pattern can also be seen in the ongoing competition between America's Boeing Corporation and the EU-based Airbus.

LESSON FOUR: Dispute settlement may not be the best forum for defending the non-trade goals of industrial policy because trade considerations weigh predominantly in panel decisions.

Canada's magazine case highlighted new challenges for trade in cultural goods at the WTO. In this case, the panel refused to find that cultural goods are qualitatively different than other consumer goods. Culture is likely going to be a large issue for the WTO in the future because cultural goods and services represent a rapidly growing portion of the global economy. Furthermore, multicultural countries, from France to India, recognize the need to balance the obvious benefits of trade with a pluralistic set of cultural policies.

In the Canadian context, free trade in cultural products is a double-edged sword because trade law exposes small Canadian cultural producers to increased intra-sectoral competition in domestic markets just as it facilitates their market access abroad. The issue is further complicated because international competition in the entertainment sector frequently requires international partnerships, which are facilitated by trade agreements. Policymakers used to look to the GATT for exemptions that would give domestic producers the breathing room they required. But now, GATT trading practice has been narrowed considerably by this panel decision. As a result,

Canada has been active at UNESCO and in intergovernmental networks looking for ways to safeguard cultural pluralism.

That Canada should take a leadership role in the protection of cultural pluralism is not surprising.[2] Despite a lucrative trade in Canadian literature and television shows, Canada remains a net importer of cultural goods. In fact, Canada consistently runs a trade deficit with all four of its largest culture trade partners: the United States, Britain, China, and France. Furthermore, with the weakness of the Doha Round, many trade watchers realize that positive movement on the culture front must occur outside the institutional umbrella of the WTO negotiations. The UNESCO Convention on the Protection and Promotion of Diversity of Cultural Expressions is the first significant step in the creation of a new institutional space in which to examine the linkages between trade, culture, and pluralism. However, progress to date has been more symbolic than real. The so-called "soft law" of declarations and conventions has had little effect on the WTO's muscular intellectual property protections, as Helfer (2004) has underlined.

LESSON FIVE: The enforcement of intellectual property (IP) rights at the WTO seems to have a chilling effect on humanitarian intervention, an effect that policymakers must overcome if the trading system is to become a true partner in international development.[3] Although the TRIPs Article 31(f) waiver of 2003 was a cautious step forward for the WTO, there is an emerging consensus that the current system does not meet the needs of developing countries. However, the WTO cannot be considered by Canadian policymakers and globalization critics to be the only, or indeed the largest, roadblock to equity when it comes to access to essential medicines.

New research shows that, even though the Doha Declaration of 2001 addressed the parallel importation rules in the Agreement on Trade-Related Aspects of Intellectual Property Rights (TRIPs), "rich countries have failed to honour their promises. Their record ranges from apathy and inaction to a dogged determination to undermine the Declaration's spirit and intent" (Malpani & Kamal-Yanni, 2006). Domestic legislation has thrown up roadblocks to the export of cheap generic drugs to African countries. After the implementation of paragraph 6 of the Doha Declaration in 2003, international pharmaceutical companies aggressively lobbied the Canadian government to restrict implementation of legislation that would take advantage of the new compulsory licensing opportunity. Despite being one of the first members to enshrine the TRIPs waiver in domestic law, Canadian generic drug producers have yet to take advantage of the new rules (with the exception of a recent Apotex submission), which are strict, cumbersome, and weighted in the interests of patent owners.

Scholars need to think more creatively about the relationships amongst trade, patents, and essential medicines, and they should examine more rigorously the theoretical linkages between these and international public health. For their part, Canadian policymakers need to broaden the relationship between foreign policy and international public health to move beyond the traditional aid programs and the more recent concern of bioterrorism.[4] International public health can and should be linked to Canada's peacekeeping efforts, post-conflict reconstruction, and the regulation of banned substances, to name a few of the possible policy linkages.[5] In the future, the WTO's relationship to public health will have an even higher profile, as national publics question the role of global governance institutions in sensitive areas of national law, such as the regulation of biotechnology. Canada can chart a leadership trajectory in this area only if government is willing to forge an independent policy that emphasizes patent equity, fair use, and equality of access to medicines for the world's poorest individuals. Despite taking an early lead on the issue of life-saving medicines for the world's poorest countries, Canada remains unable to balance global need with private profit.

These lessons are certainly not hard to absorb, and, indeed, several of them have likely already influenced decisions coming out of Foreign Affairs and International Trade Canada. Lesson five, in particular, will be difficult for Canada's policy bureaucrats to put into practice because it places IP enforcement at apparent odds with humanitarian assistance. Most important, Canada has learned that WTO litigation is not a replacement for intellectual leadership and policy innovation if a country wants to get the most out of multilateral participation. The WTO's rules may not always be the right rules, but they lay the groundwork for a more comprehensive and effective rule of law. History has proven that Canada's comparative lack of economic power has been a catalyst for deeper multilateral engagement. Canadian policymakers can use this engagement to create a better balance between Canada's position on the periphery of power politics and the national goals of achieving diversified markets and a more balanced relationship with the country's largest trading partner.

TRADING INTO THE FUTURE

The Doha Round of trade negotiations has the express purpose of opening markets to developing nations. The WTO Secretariat has placed much emphasis on the benefits of trade for developing nations, yet these countries still face many barriers to effective participation in global trade. Non-tariff barriers erected by developed countries to shield sensitive sectors have effectively shut developing nations out of lucrative markets for agricultural products in North America and Europe. For example, a tariff and quota system protects Canada's dairy industry, and, even if the current trade round is concluded successfully, it will only marginally lessen the steep tariffs that protect dairy producers in the developed world.

Other development issues cut across global trade rules, including the need for effective economic development strategies within the poorest nations, workable poverty reduction programs at the international level, and dependable and effective foreign aid programs delivered by industrialized nations. In the mid 1990s, it was conventional wisdom that free trade raises the incomes of poor countries and can be a potent engine of economic development. But further research has shown how simple and misleading this assumption can be if it is not subjected to rigorous empirical scrutiny. In fact, trade has a relatively small impact on economic growth, and it must be calibrated with appropriate social and industrial policies to be effective (Rodrik, 2003). The fact that HIV/AIDS continues to ravage portions of Africa, Asia, and Latin America, only highlights the significant work that needs to be done to build infrastructure in developing nations before many of the WTO's members can use the system effectively to grow out of poverty.

Nevertheless, small countries continue to join the multilateral trading order. Even inadequate rules are better than no rules at all. Developing nations know that, in the long run, membership in the multilateral system must be a part of their economic policies and trade strategies, even if there are few benefits in the short term. Their membership is either a form of global optimism, which bodes well for the future of international cooperation, or it is the result of the structural power of industrialized nations that have championed the WTO. The jury is still out. But the proliferation of regional and bilateral trade deals over the past 15 years suggests that global economic integration is not necessarily a top-down phenomenon. Beyond the trade realm, supranational legal organizations are growing in popularity because they are the most effective means available to orchestrate state action and coordinate policies in an era in which technological innovation has massively increased the intensity and scope of global flows of people, money, and information. International organizations allow states to achieve goals they cannot achieve on a decentralized basis; the remarkable postwar reduction of industrial tariffs is a case in point (Abbott & Snidal, 1998).

In the summer of 2006, the Doha Round finally ran out of gas and stalled. By February 2007, negotiations were back on their feet, but limping badly. During informal discussions among leading trade ministers in 2008, few of the many divides between rich and poor countries were bridged, and hopes for a conclusion to the round diminished markedly. During the last year of the George W. Bush administration, trade watchers began to discuss the possibility of a pause in the round, if only until the Obama administration could take effective leadership. Those hopes were derailed by massive bank collapses on Wall Street at the end of 2008. Now, not even a miracle can deliver on the promises of the Doha development agenda of 2001, and there are no trade boosters willing to suggest that the current global economic system is capable of sustaining international development throughout the next century. When a wide-angle lens is applied, it now appears that the new millennium has been marked by economic uncertainty, political violence, and a rising tide of social instability that is one of the negative outcomes of three decades of faulty international policies (Wade, 2001). Clearly, Canada is long overdue for a public discussion about its trade interests, its foreign policy goals, and its development priorities at home and abroad.

Canada has much to offer the emerging economic powers in the developing world, and they have much to teach Canada. In structural terms, Canada's historical trade policy challenges — resource dependence, the struggle for industrial independence, and the search for an effective monetary policy — bear a striking resemblance to the challenges facing many developing countries such as Brazil, India, Korea, Vietnam, and, to a lesser extent, China. These countries are developing unique regulatory models in the shadow of the great trading partners. And, just as in many emerging economies, Canada's industrial policies have always rested uncomfortably beside heavy exports of raw materials and agricultural products. Using the WTO to craft the right policy approach may yet be essential to Canada's strategy of multilateral relationship management and trade diversification. Likewise, the WTO could benefit from a strong, large trading nation that takes up the call for a trading order in the service of development and poverty reduction. In fact, such a member would also be working in the service of the WTO because, currently, the biggest players seem to be relatively disinterested in the fact that the system does not work well for many, if not most, developing country members.

Canada needs to build trade ties in the global south, and developing countries need a partner willing to cut farm support and open its domestic markets to agri-food products. Canada is the world's fourth largest agri-food exporter and one of the top four agricultural subsidizers. Canada needs to maintain its agricultural industries but not through current practices that discriminate against developing producers and dump surpluses on world markets. Canada has the makings of a natural partner for many developing economies in Latin America in particular. For example, Canada and Brazil have a mutually advantageous trade relationship, which, on Canada's part, has grown significantly. According to *Canada's International Policy Statement* (Canada. Department of Foreign Affairs and International Trade, 2005), foreign direct investment in Brazil has increased by almost 300 per cent in the last decade, from $2 billion in 1993 to $7.6 billion in 2003. Fractious disputes such as the one involving regional jets damage Canada's reputation in developing markets and may harm trade diversification priorities.

This is not to say that "doing the rules" is an exercise in futility. Rather, I am arguing that Canadian policymakers need to decide on a trade strategy that works with both a "Canadian values" brand of foreign policy as well as with Canadian trading interests. They need not fear that Canada's continental position precludes a deeper and more robust engagement with the developing world. Douglass North (2005) has shown that economic reality is what countries make of it. He means that economic change is a process that begins with altering our perceptions of the current economic situation and then moving to change our institutions and policies in order to meet our new economic goals. Creating an equitable and orderly system is an ongoing challenge to which the WTO system is only a partial answer. A more effective rule of international law is in the interest of all members. But it will take creativity, judgment, and courage to create a system that benefits all of its members. If properly aligned, Canada's humanitarian values and strategic trading priorities make it a natural institutional reformer for a more effective trading order.

Notes

1. For specifics of the deal, see the BC Ministry of Forests and Range's information sheet entitled "Basic terms of a Canada-United States agreement on softwood lumber," retrieved October 29, 2009 from http://www.for.gov.bc.ca/HET/Softwood/Term%20Sheet%20Apr%2027%202006.pdf.

2. In November 2001, UNESCO's General Conference, composed of 190 member countries, acclaimed the Universal Declaration on Cultural Diversity. This declaration, while not legally binding, reaffirmed the centrality of culture to national identity, human freedom, and southern development. The UNESCO Universal Declaration on Cultural Diversity is the first step towards the creation of an independent instrument for defending cultural diversity. In particular, articles 3, 8, 9, and 11 of the declaration provide a very different understanding of trade and culture from that promoted by the WTO, advocating cultural diversity as a factor in development and asserting the unique nature of cultural goods and services and the central role of the state in defining and implementing cultural policy. The more recent Convention on the Protection and Promotion of the Diversity of Cultural Expressions, adopted at the end of 2005, is also an important step in the ongoing political project to create a space for the incubation of alternate regulatory models to govern the large, and growing, trade in cultural goods and services. France and Canada, the convention's sponsors, believe that

the use of such multilateral mechanisms to affirm their sovereign rights to protect cultural diversity will ultimately strengthen their position on cultural trade
at the WTO. Both countries, like many European and Asian nations, use subsidies to support domestic cultural producers, and these cultural and industrial
policies are increasingly under attack. That the most recent convention was
drafted and adopted with only the United States and Israel voting against it is a
powerful signal that free trade is not eroding state authority nor is market competition replacing governmental responsibility for cultural pluralism. Read the
full declarations at www.unesco.org/culture.

3. For example, see the report of the World Health Organization's Commission on
Intellectual Property Rights, Innovation, and Public Health, which is entitled
Public Health: Innovation and Intellectual Property Rights and is available from
www.who.int/intellectualproperty.

4. For example, McInnes and Lee (2006) underscore the emerging relationship
between foreign and security policies and public health. To date, the relationship
between public health and international security has been limited to issues such
as southern bioterror threats against northern targets and the possible links
between AIDs and failed states. Nevertheless, the AIDS crisis, secure and safe
food and water, and even tobacco control initiatives cannot be properly understood as mutually exclusive of current foreign policies, poverty reduction, and
international security goals.

5. The downside of the securitization of HIV is that it pushes responses to HIV
away from civil society and towards the military and intelligence services. This
can undermine international attempts to address the pandemic by appealing to
national interest rather than to the promotion of international health and multilateral cooperation. See Elbe's (2006) discussion for an in-depth analysis of the
ethical dimensions of security and health pandemics.

Table A.1. *Comparing GATT Diplomacy and WTO Rules*

Features	GATT 1947	WTO
Governance model	Regime management model	Trade stakeholder model
Dispute settlement mechanism	No provision for formal, juridical dispute settlement; emphasis on diplomatic methods of consultation and consensus (evolving from the provisions of Article XXII, XXIII)	WTO Dispute Settlement Understanding (DSU)
Source of panellists	Mostly junior to middle-level trade diplomats or retired trade diplomats (mostly without formal legal training), very much influenced by the Secretariat	Panel: "well-qualified governmental and/or non governmental individuals"; Appellate Body: seven "persons of recognized authority, with demonstrated expertise in law, international trade, and the covered agreements generally"
Time limit for dispute settlement	No hard time limits on consultation, responses to requests for panels, and panel proceedings and rulings "A reasonable time" was the guiding time restriction for the GATT system	Time limits provided for each step of dispute settlement (e.g., panel report circulated to DSB in a maximum of nine months after the establishment of a panel)
Appeal proceeding	None	Innovation of appeal
Adoption of ruling	Adoption of a ruling depends on the consensus of all contracting parties (making ruling adoption difficult, if not impossible, due to opposition of losing party)	Rejection of a ruling depends on the consensus of all contracting parties (making ruling adoption almost automatic)

How Does Dispute Settlement Work?

In *Bleak House*, Charles Dickens's classic tale of greed and legal turpitude, young Richard Carstone spends his life, happiness, and finally his health in a court battle for a family inheritance that is ultimately consumed in legal fees. The courts, it seems, are an expensive and uncertain route to justice. Governments also know that intractable disputes can eat up valuable resources and drag on for years. The WTO's Dispute Settlement Body was created in order to improve the GATT's more informal system of dispute settlement. The many rules and procedures, although they may seem arcane, are designed to expedite lengthy international disputes and hold parties to account when their actions are found to contravene international law.

THE DISPUTE SETTLEMENT PROCESS

The objective of the new dispute settlement process is to provide security and predictability to the multilateral trading system. The process is defined in the Understanding on Rules and Procedures Governing the Settlement of Disputes, more commonly called the Dispute Settlement Understanding (DSU). The DSU provides for both a panel and an appeals process in an attempt to systematically preserve the rights and obligations of the members covered under agreements and to clarify the existing provisions of those agreements in accordance with customary rules of interpretation of public international law. Most important, the new system aims for prompt settlement of situations in which a member considers that its benefits of membership are being impaired by another member. Although the system closely resembles litigation in civil court, countries in dispute are encouraged to consult each other in order to settle "out of court" at any stage in the proceedings, and, at all stages, the WTO director-general is available to offer his or her good offices, to mediate, or to help achieve a diplomatic outcome.

Dispute Consultations

When one country adopts a trade policy measure or takes some action that at least one fellow WTO member considers to be breaking the WTO agreements or to be a failure to live up to obligations, a claim may be made based on any of the multilateral trade agreements included in the annexes to the Agreement Establishing the World Trade Organization. In bringing a case to the WTO, it is understood that all members will engage in a good faith effort to resolve the dispute. Occasionally, third parties, not directly involved, may intervene in the dispute. When another member has a substantial trade interest in the consultations being held, it may notify the Dispute Settlement Body of its desire to take part in consultations within 10 days of the original request for consultations; if this request is not accepted (because the member's substantial interest was deemed to be not well founded) that member is free to request its own consultations.

Table A.2. *The WTO Agreement*

Agreement Establishing the World Trade Organization

a) *Multilateral trade agreements*
Annex 1A: Multilateral agreements on trade in goods, e.g.,
    General Agreement on Tariffs and Trade (GATT)
    Agreement on Sanitary and Phytosanitary Measures
    Agreement on Trade-Related Aspects of Investment Measures (TRIMs)
    Agreement on Subsidies and Countervailing Measures (SCM)

Annex 1B: General Agreement on Trade in Services
Annex 1C: Agreement on Trade-Related Aspects of Intellectual
    Property Rights
Annex 2: Understanding on Rules and Procedures Governing the
    Settlement of Disputes
Annex 3: Trade Policy Review Mechanism

b) *Plurilateral trade agreements*
Annex 4: Agreement on Trade in Civil Aircraft
    Agreement on Government Procurement
    International Dairy Agreement
    International Bovine Meat Agreement

Multiple Complainants

According to the Understanding on Rules and Procedures Governing the Settlement of Disputes, a single panel should be established to examine multiple complaints related to the same matter whenever feasible. Use of a single rather than multiple panels should not impair the rights of the parties, however, who may request separate reports. If more than one panel is established to examine complaints related to the same matter, wherever possible, the same panellists serve on the panels and the dispute process timetables are harmonized.

Developing Countries

Developing country complaints are treated according to the special and differential treatment accorded under the WTO Agreement. If a developing country member brings a complaint against a developed country member, the complainant may invoke old rules with extended time limits. Also, members are cautioned to exercise due restraint when raising matters involving a least developed country member.

The Consultation Process

A country must reply to a request for consultation from another member within 10 days and enter into consultations within 30 days of that request. If these time limits are not met, the complainant may request immediate establishment of a panel. If consultations fail, parties can also ask the WTO director-general to mediate or try to help in any other way—parties may voluntarily agree to follow alternative means of dispute settlement including good offices, conciliation, mediation, and arbitration. During consultations, members are asked to give special attention to the particular problems of developing countries. For example, if consultations involve a developing country, parties or the panel chair or the DSB may decide to extend some time limits (as per DSU Article 12:10).

If consultations do not yield a solution after 60 days (20 days for urgent situations), the complaining country can ask for a panel to be appointed. When the dispute is not settled through consultations, the DSU requires the establishment of a panel, at the latest, at the meeting following that at which a request is made, unless the DSB decides by consensus against establishing a panel. The responding country can block the creation of a panel once, but when the DSB meets for a second time, the appointment of a panel can no longer be blocked (unless there is a consensus against appointing the panel). The DSB has the sole authority to establish panels of experts to consider the case at the WTO.

Panel Composition

Panellists can be chosen for up to about 50 days after the DSB establishes a panel (DSU Article 8). When parties do not agree on the composition of the panel within 20 days, the decision can be made by the WTO director-general. Panels contain three (occasionally five) experts, with diverse backgrounds and experience, from countries not party to the dispute. The WTO Secretariat maintains a list of experts satisfying the criteria, and it proposes nominations for the panel, which parties to the dispute are asked not to oppose except for compelling reasons. Panellists serve in their individual capacities; they cannot receive instructions from any government.

Qualified panellists include any governmental or non-governmental individual who has served on or presented a case to a WTO panel, represented a member country at the WTO or one of the contracting parties of GATT 1947, served on a council or committee of any covered agreement or in the WTO Secretariat, taught or published on international trade law or policy, or served as a senior trade policy official of a member country. When a dispute involves a developing country member, that member may request that the panel include at least one panellist from another developing country member.

Panel Examination

All panel deliberations are confidential and drafted without disputing parties present. The opinions expressed by the panel are anonymous. Before the first hearing, each side in the dispute presents its case in writing to the panel. At the first hearing, the case for the complaining country and the defence of the responding country are heard, along with third-party submissions. The countries involved submit written rebuttals and present oral arguments at the panel's second meeting. If one side raises scientific or other technical matters, the panel may consult experts or appoint an expert review group to prepare an advisory report. Normally, there is a presumption that a breach of the rules has an adverse effect on other parties in the dispute, and, in such cases, it is the responsibility of the member against whom the complaint has been brought to rebut the charge (DSU Article 3:8). Regardless, it is the panel's responsibility to make an objective assessment of the facts and of the applicability of relevant agreements (DSU Article 11).

The first draft of the panel report does not include findings and conclusions. The panel submits the descriptive sections (facts and arguments) of its report to the two sides, giving them two weeks to comment. Then the panel submits an interim report, including its findings and conclusions to the two sides, giving them one week to ask for a review. If a review is not requested, the interim report will become the final panel report. The final panel report should be issued to the parties within six months from panel's composition, or in three months if the case is urgent (e.g., if perishables are involved). The final report is submitted to both sides, and members having objections to the panel report are allowed to make them ten days prior to the DSB meeting at which time the report will be considered (DSU Article 16:2). If the dispute involves a developing country, the report must indicate how special and differential treatment provisions for developing countries have been taken into account (DSU Article 12:11). Three weeks after a final report is submitted to the DSB, it is submitted to all WTO members.

Report Adoption

Panel rulings are endorsed automatically by the WTO's full membership. Parties to the dispute may participate fully in the consideration of the panel report, and their views will be fully recorded (DSU Article 16:3). The DSB has sole authority to accept or reject a panel's findings or the results of an appeal. The panel report becomes the DSB's ruling or recommendation within 60 days unless a consensus rejects it or unless one of the parties notifies the DSB of its intention to appeal. (This report adoption procedure is opposite to that originally outlined by GATT, which required a consensus to accept a ruling and, consequently, allowed losing parties to block rulings.) As for panel recommendations, when an inconsistent measure is found, the panel recommends that the member bring it into conformity with the covered agreements; the panel may also suggest ways of implementation. However, the panel cannot add to or diminish the rights and obligations provided in the covered agreements.

Appellate Review

Both sides can appeal (and in some cases, both do), but third parties may not appeal. Appeals must be based on points of law such as legal interpretation; they cannot re-examine existing evidence or examine new evidence. The DSB establishes a permanent seven-member standing Appellate Body (AB), which hears appeals from panel cases. AB members are appointed for a four-year term, and each person may be reappointed once. Appellate Body members are persons of recognized authority, with demonstrated expertise in law, international trade, and the subject matters of the agreements, and they are unaffiliated with any government. Each appeal is heard by three members of the AB. Proceedings are confidential, and the opinions expressed are anonymous.

The Appellate Body can uphold, modify, or reverse the panel's legal findings and conclusions. When inconsistent measures are found, the Appellate Body recommends that the member come into conformity with the covered agreements; like the panel, the AB may also suggest ways of implementation.

The Appellate Body cannot add to or diminish the rights and obligations provided in the covered agreements. The DSB accepts or rejects an appeals report within 30 days. Again, rejection is only possible by consensus.

Implementation

The DSB monitors implementation until the issue is resolved (DSU Article 21). Prompt compliance with recommendations or rulings of the DSB is essential to the efficiency and effectiveness of the system. The losing party must state its intentions to follow the recommendations of the panel report at a DSB meeting held within 30 days of the report's adoption (DSU Article 21:3). If complying with the recommendation immediately proves impracticable, the member will be given a reasonable period of time to do so. By definition, a "reasonable period of time" may be the time proposed by the member concerned and approved by the DSB; the time mutually agreed to by the parties within 45 days of the report's adoption; or the time decided by arbitration, which must take place within 90 days of the report's adoption.

Status Reports

The member ruled against must provide the DSB with an implementation progress report ten days prior to each DSB meeting. In the implementation of rulings against developing country members, the DSB considers the trade coverage of measures complained of and the impact on the economy of the developing country member. When there is disagreement as to the existence of a measure taken to comply with the recommendations and rulings of the WTO or with the consistency of such a measure with the panel's decision, the original panel may be consulted — in recourse to Article 21.5 of the Dispute Settlement Understanding.

It should be noted that neither compensation nor suspension of concessions is preferred to the full implementation of the panel report. But, if a losing country fails to act within the agreed-upon time, it must enter into negotiations with the complaining party to determine a mutually acceptable compensation. Tariff reductions in areas of particular interest to the complaining side are just one example of such a compensation. However, compensation should only be used if the immediate withdrawal of the measure is impracticable, and then only as a temporary measure pending withdrawal of that measure.

At the same time, compensation remains voluntary, and, if granted, it should be consistent with the covered agreements. If after 20 days no satisfactory compensation is agreed upon, the complaining side may ask the DSB for permission to impose limited trade sanctions in the form of a suspension of concessions and obligations to the other country, but only until the inconsistent measure is brought into line with covered agreements or a mutually satisfactory diplomatic solution is reached. Disagreements over proposed level or type of suspension may be referred to arbitration.

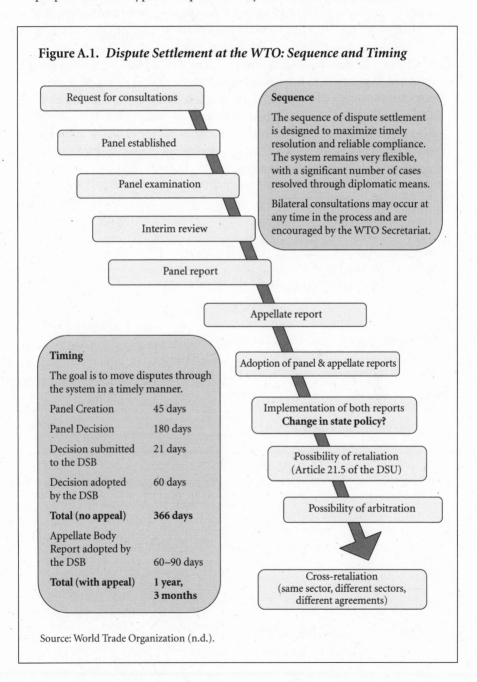

Figure A.1. *Dispute Settlement at the WTO: Sequence and Timing*

Request for consultations

Panel established

Panel examination

Interim review

Panel report

Appellate report

Sequence

The sequence of dispute settlement is designed to maximize timely resolution and reliable compliance. The system remains very flexible, with a significant number of cases resolved through diplomatic means.

Bilateral consultations may occur at any time in the process and are encouraged by the WTO Secretariat.

Adoption of panel & appellate reports

Implementation of both reports **Change in state policy?**

Possibility of retaliation (Article 21.5 of the DSU)

Possibility of arbitration

Cross-retaliation (same sector, different sectors, different agreements)

Timing

The goal is to move disputes through the system in a timely manner.

Panel Creation	45 days
Panel Decision	180 days
Decision submitted to the DSB	21 days
Decision adopted by the DSB	60 days
Total (no appeal)	**366 days**
Appellate Body Report adopted by the DSB	60–90 days
Total (with appeal)	**1 year, 3 months**

Source: World Trade Organization (n.d.).

Sanctions

In principle, sanctions should be imposed in the same economic sector as the dispute. However, if this is not practical or if it would not be effective, the sanctions can be imposed in a different sector, as long as it is a sector covered by the same agreement. Only if circumstances are very serious should action be taken under another agreement, an action practically unheard of at the WTO. The objective is to minimize the chance of retaliation spilling into unrelated sectors. When implementing decisions against developing countries, members should exercise restraint in asking for compensation or in seeking authorization to suspend obligations or concessions. If no agreement on compensation can be reached, the DSB has the power to authorize retaliation pending full implementation — including cross-retaliation involving other sectors or other agreements.

References and Recommended Readings

Abbott, F.M. (2003). Bob Hudec as chair of the Canada–Generic Pharmaceuticals Panel: The WTO gets something right. *Journal of International Economic Law, 6*(3), 733–737.

Abbott, F.M. (2005). The WTO medicines decision: World pharmaceutical trade and the protection of public health. *American Journal of International Law, 99*(2), 317–358.

Abbott, K.M., & Snidal, D. (1998). Why states act through formal international institutions. *Journal of Conflict Resolution, 42*(1), 3–32.

Abbott, P.C., & Kallio, P. K. S. (1996). Implications of game theory for international agriculture trade. *American Journal of Agricultural Economics, 78*, 738–744.

Acheson, K., & Maule, C. (1999). *Much ado about culture: North American trade disputes* (R. M. Stern, Ed.). Studies in International Economics. Ann Arbor, MI: University of Michigan Press.

Akerlof, G.A., & Shiller, R. J. (2009). *Animal spirits: How human psychology drives the economy and why it matters for global capitalism.* Princeton, NJ: Princeton University Press.

Alden, E., & Minder, R. (2004, October 4). Dogfight at the WTO: The US and EU step up their battle over aircraft subsidies. *Financial Times*, p. 17.

Allee, T.L., & Huth, P.K. (2006). Legitimizing dispute settlement: International legal rulings as domestic political cover. *American Political Science Review, 100*(2), 219–234.

Alston, L.J. (2005). The "case" for case studies in political economy. *The Political Economist: Newsletter of the Section on Political Economy, American Political Science Association, 12*(4), 1, 8, 10, 14–19, 21.

Alter, K.J. (2003). Resolving or exacerbating disputes? The WTO's new dispute resolution system. *International Affairs, 79*(4), 783–800.

Anderson, G. (2003). The compromise of embedded liberalism, American trade remedy law, and Canadian softwood lumber: Can't we all just get along? *Canadian Foreign Policy, 10*(2), 87–108.

Annand, M. (2000). State trading enterprises: A Canadian perspective. *Estey Centre Journal of International Law and Trade Policy, 2*(1), 36–50.

Antkiewicz, A., & Whalley, J. (2005). *BRICSAM and the non-WTO* (CIG Working Paper No. 3). Waterloo, ON: The Centre for International Governance Innovation. Retrieved June 12, 2006, from www.cigionline.org.

Arthurs, H. (2003). *The hollowing out of corporate Canada? How the microphysics of power may shape the fate of nations.* Cambridge, MA: Harvard University, Weatherhead Center for International Affairs.

Axworthy, L. (2003). *Navigating a new world: Canada's global future.* Toronto: Vintage Canada.

Bagwell, K., & Staiger, R.W. (2006). *What do trade negotiators negotiate about? Empirical evidence from the World Trade Organization.* Cambridge, MA: National Bureau of Economic Research.

Baldwin, R.E. (2003). *Openness and growth: What's the empirical relationship?* Cambridge, MA: National Bureau of Economic Research.

Banting, K. (1997). The social policy divide: The welfare state in Canada and the United States. In K. Banting, G. Hoberg, & R. Simeon (Eds.), *Degrees of freedom: Canada and the United States in a changing world* (pp. 267–309). Montreal: McGill-Queen's University Press.

Barton, J.H., Goldstein, J.L., Josling, T.E., & Steinberg, R.H. (2006). *The evolution of the trade regime: Politics, law, and the economics of the GATT and the WTO.* Princeton, NJ: Princeton University Press.

Baxter, M., & Kouparitsas, M.A. (2006). *What determines bilateral trade flows?* Cambridge, MA: National Bureau of Economic Research.

Bello, W., & Kwa, A. (2003, May 12–13). *The stalemate in the WTO and the crisis of the globalist project: Update on the World Trade Organization and global trends.* Paper presented at the Hemispheric and Global Assembly Against the FTAA and the WTO, Mexico City. Retrieved June 11, 2006, from http://www.tni.org/detail_page.phtml?page=archives_bello_globaltrends.

Bernier, I. (2000). *Catalogue of international principles pertaining to culture.* Quebec City: Faculty of Law, Laval University.

Bernier, I. (2001). *A new international instrument on cultural diversity: Questions and answers.* Retrieved August 16, 2004, from the International Network for Cultural Diversity website: http://www.incd.net/docs/NIICD.htm.

Bernstein, W.J. (2008). *A splendid exchange: How trade shaped the world.* New York: Atlantic Monthly Press.

Bhagwati, J. (20007, October 8). *The consensus for free trade among economists: Has it frayed?* Lecture given at the World Trade Organization. Retrieved October 28, 2009 from www.wto.org/english/news_e/news07_e/bhagwati_oct07_e.htm.

Blonigen, B.A., & Bown, C.P. (2001, October). *Antidumping and retaliation threats* (NBER Working Paper No. 8576). Cambridge, MA: National Bureau of Economic Research. Retrieved November 4, 2009, from http://www.nber.org/antidump/.

Bora, B., Lloyd, P.J., & Pangestu, M. (2000). *Industrial policy and the WTO*. Geneva: United Nations Conference on Trade and Development (UNCTAD).

Bourgeois, J.H.J. (2001). Some reflections on the WTO dispute settlement system from a practitioner's perspective. *Journal of International Economic Law, 4*, 145–154.

Bourgeois, J.H.J., & Messerlin, P. A.(1998). The European Community's experience. In R. Lawrence (Ed.), *Brookings Trade Forum 1998* (pp. 127–146). Washington, DC: Brookings Institution Press.

Bown, C.P. (2004). On the economic success of GATT/WTO dispute settlement. *Review of Economics and Statistics, 86*(3), 811–823.

Brimeyer, B.L. (2001). Bananas, beef and compliance in the World Trade Organization: The inability of the WTO dispute settlement process to achieve compliance from superpower nations. *Minnesota Journal of Global Trade, 10*(1), 133–168.

Bronckers, M.C.E.J. (2001). More power to the WTO? *Journal of Economic Literature, 4*(4), 41–65.

Bull, H. (1977). *The anarchical society: A study of order in world politics*. London: Macmillan.

Burleton, D., & Apollonova, N. (2006). *Canada's image as a global resource giant: More than just perception . . . It's a reality*. Toronto: Toronto Dominion Bank Financial Group.

Byers, M. (2007). *Intent for a nation: What is Canada for?* Toronto: Douglas & Mcintyre.

Canada. Department of Foreign Affairs and International Trade. (2005). *Canada's international policy statement: A role of pride and influence in the world*. Ottawa: Government of Canada.

Canadian Generic Pharmaceutical Association. (2004). Bill C-9, the Jean Crétien Pledge to Africa. *News Releases*. Retrieved October 28, 2008 from the Canadian Generic Pharmaceutical Association website: www.canadiangenerics.ca.

Canadian Generic Pharmaceutical Association. (2008, April 16). Overview of Canada's generic pharmaceutical industry. *News Releases*. Retrieved November 5, 2009 from the Canadian Generic Pharmaceutical Association website: www.canadiangenerics.ca.

Canadian Intellectual Property Office. (2004). *Annual report 2003–2004: Delivering quality services.* Ottawa: Author. Retrieved October 28, 2009, from http://www.cipo.ic.gc.ca/eic/site/cipointernet-internetopic.nsf/eng/h_wr00094.html.

Canadian Wheat Board. (2008). *A history of U.S. trade challenges.* Retrieved October 21, 2009, from http://www.cwb.ca/public/en/hot/trade/popups/trade_history.jsp.

Capgemini US LCC. (2005). *9th Annual Merrill Lynch/Capgemini World Wealth Report* New York: Author. Retrieved November 5, 2006, from http://www.us.capgemini.com/.

Carney, D. (2000, September 19). WTO Appellate Body rules that Canada's 17-year patent term violates TRIPs. *Tech Law Journal.* Retrieved February 21, 2008, from http://www.techlawjournal.com/trade/20000919.asp.

Carter, C.A., & Loyns, R.M.A. (1996.) *The economics of single desk selling of western Canadian grain.* Edmonton, AB: Alberta Ministry of Agriculture and Rural Development. Retrieved October 29, 2009, from http://www1.agric.gov.ab.ca/$department/deptdocs.nsf/all/agc2248.

Chakravarthi, R. (2000). *Canada, Brazil Seek Modus Vivendi on Trade Retaliation.* Retrieved February 21, 2005 from the Third World Network website: http://www.twnside.org.sg/title/vivendi.htm.

Charnovitz, S. (2002). Triangulating the World Trade Organization. *American Journal of International Law, 96*(1), 28–55.

Charnovitz, S. (2005). An analysis of Pascal Lamy's proposal on collective preferences. *Journal of International Economic Law, 8*(2), 449–472.

Chase, S. (2004, April 21). Bill on cheap drugs for poor countries may still impede generic firms, critics say. *The Globe and Mail,* p. A5.

Chayes, A., & Chayes, A.H. (1995). *The new sovereignty: Compliance with international regulatory agreements.* Cambridge, MA: Harvard University Press.

Ciuriak, D. (2005). Antidumping at 100 years and counting: A Canadian perspective. *The World Economy, 28*(5), 641–649.

Clarkson, S. (2002). *Uncle Sam and us: Globalization, neo-Conservatism and the Canadian state.* Toronto: University of Toronto Press.

Clemens, M.A., & Williamson, J.G.(2001). *A tariff-growth paradox? Protection's impact around the world 1875–1997.* Washington, DC: National Bureau of Economic Research.

Cooper, A.F. (2004). *Tests of global governance: Canadian diplomacy and United Nations world conferences.* New York: United Nations University Press.

Cooper, A.F. (2008) Thinking outside the box in the Canada–Mexico relations: From convenience to commitment. In D. Drache (Ed.), *Big-picture realities: Canada and Mexico at the crossroads* (pp. 237–250). Waterloo, ON: Wilfrid Laurier University Press.

Cox, R.W., & Schechter, M.G. (2002). *Political economy of a plural world: Critical reflections on power, morals, and civilization*. London: Routledge.

Cross, P. (2007). The new underground economy of subsoil resources: No longer hewers of wood and drawers of water. *Canadian Economic Observer, 29*(10), 3.1–3.12.

Cross, P., & Ghanem, Z. (2005). Canada's natural resource exports. *Canadian Economic Observer, 18*(5), 3.1–3.7.

Currie, J.H. (2001). *Public international law*. Toronto, ON: Irwin Law.

Cutler, A.C. (2001). Critical reflections on the Westphalian assumptions of international law and organization: A crisis of legitimacy. *Review of International Studies, 27*(2), 133–150.

Cutler, A.C. (2003). *Private power and global authority: Transnational merchant law in the global political economy*. Cambridge: Cambridge University Press.

D' Cruz, J., & Gastle, C.M. (2002, February). *Canada-Brazil relations: An expedited arbitral mechanism may be required to resolve the WTO aircraft from Brazil–Canada dispute*. Saskatoon, SK: Estey Centre for Law and Economics in International Trade. Retrieved October 28, 2009, from http://www.esteycentre.ca/canadabrazil.htm.

De Meza, D. (1989). Not even strategic trade theory justifies export subsidies. *Oxford Economic Papers, 41*(4), 720–736.

Destler, I.M. (2005). *American trade politics* (4th ed.). Washington, DC: Institute for International Economics.

Dickins, A. (2006). The evolution of international political economy. *International Affairs, 82*(3), 479–492.

Doern, G.B., & Sharaput, M. (2000). *Canadian intellectual property: The politics of innovating institutions and interests*. Toronto, ON: University of Toronto Press.

Dollar, D., & Kraay, A. (2001, June). *Trade growth and poverty*. World Bank Policy Research Working Paper No. 2615. Washington, DC: World Bank Development Research Group.

Dorland, M. (Ed.). (1996). *The cultural industries in Canada: Problems, policies, and prospects*. Toronto: James Lorimer & Company.

Drache, D., (Ed.). (2001). *The market or the public domain: Global governance and the asymmetry of power*. London: Routledge.

Drache, D. (2004). *Borders matter: Homeland security and the search for North America*. Halifax, NS: Fernwood Publishing.

Drache, D., & Froese, M.D.(2006). Globalization, world trade, and the cultural commons: Identity, citizenship, and pluralism. *New Political Economy, 11*(3), 359–380.

Drache, D., & Froese, M.D. (2008). *Defiant publics: The unprecedented reach of the global citizen*. London: Polity Press.

Drache, D., & Froese, M.D. (2008a). Omens and threats in the Doha Round: The decline of multilateralism. *Man and Development, 30*(2), 1–28.

Drope, J. M., & Hansen, W.L . (2006). Antidumping's happy birthday? *The World Economy, 28*(4), 459–472.

Dubinsky, L. (1996). Periodical publishing. In M. Dorland (Ed.), *The cultural industries in Canada: problems, policies, and prospects* (pp. 35–59). Toronto, ON: James Lorimer & Company.

Duer, A. (2008). Bringing economic interests back into the study of EU trade policy-making. *British Journal of Politics and International Relations, 10*(1), 27–45.

Duy, V. (2001). *A brief history of the Canadian patent system*. Ottawa: Canadian Biotechnology Advisory Committee, Steering Committee on Intellectual Property and the Patenting of Higher Life Forms.

Ehlermann, C.-D., & Lockhart, N. (2004). Standard of review in WTO law. *Journal of International Economic Law, 7*(3), 491–521.

Eichengreen, B., & Irwin, D.A. (1993). *Trade blocs, currency blocs, and the disintegration of world trade in the 1930s*. Cambridge, MA: National Bureau of Economic Research.

Elbe, S. (2006). Should HIV/AIDS be securitized? The ethical dilemmas of linking HIV/AIDS and security. *International Studies Quarterly, 50*, 119–144.

European Association of Aerospace Industries (AECMA). (2003). *The European aerospace industry: Facts & figures, 2002*. Brussels: Author.

Fatoumata, J., & Kwa A. (2003). *Behind the scenes at the WTO: The real world of international trade negotiations*. New York: Zed Books.

Fioretos, O. (2001). The domestic sources of multilateral preferences: Varieties of capitalism in the European Community. In P. A. Hall & D. Soskice (Eds.), *Varieties of capitalism: The institutional foundations of comparative advantage* (pp. 213–244). Oxford: Oxford University Press.

Foreign Affairs and International Trade Canada. (2009). *Softwood lumber*. Retrieved October 29, 2009, from http://www.international.gc.ca/controls-controles/softwood-bois_oeuvre/index.aspx?menu_id=19&menu=R.

Frieden, J., & Martin, L.L. (2002). International political economy: Global and domestic interactions. In I. Katznelson & H.V. Milner (Eds.), *Political science: The state of the discipline* (pp. 118–146). New York: W.W. Norton and Company.

Furtan, H.W. (2005). Transformative change in agriculture: The Canadian Wheat Board. *Estey Centre Journal of International Law and Trade Policy, 6*(2), 95–107.

Gagné, G. (2003). The Canada–US softwood lumber dispute: A test case for the development of international rules. *International Journal, 58*(3), 335–368.

Gattinger, M. (2002, May 29–31). *Globalization, two-level negotiations and symbolic policy: The case of Canada's cultural industries in trade*. Paper presented at the

Annual Conference of the Canadian Political Science Association, University of Toronto, Toronto, ON.

Gibson, G. (2006, October 17). The "softwood sellout agreement" is not the final word. *The Globe and Mail*, p. A21.

Gill, S. (1995). Constitutionalizing inequality and the clash of globalizations. *Millennium, 23*(3), 399–423.

Glassman, James K. The axis of IP evil. *Capitalism Magazine*. Retrieved January 29, 2010, from http://www.capmag.com/article.asp?10=4356.

Government of Canada. (1998). Order amending the schedule to the Customs Tariff (certain periodicals). *Canada Gazette, 132*(23), SOR/98-543.

Grant, G. (1965). *Lament for a nation: The defeat of Canadian nationalism*. Montreal: McGill-Queen's University Press.

Grant, P.S., & Wood, C. (2004). *Blockbusters and trade wars: Popular culture in a globalized world*. Toronto: Douglas & McIntyre.

Hadekel, P. (2004). *Silent partners: Taxpayers and the bankrolling of Bombardier*. Toronto: Key Porter Books.

Haggart, R. (2005, October 28). Everything you always wanted to know about softwood but were afraid to ask. *The Globe and Mail*, p. A23.

Hall, P.A., & Soskice, D. (Eds.). (2001). *Varieties of capitalism: The institutional foundations of comparative advantage*. New York: Oxford University Press.

Hart, M. (1997). Twenty years of Canadian tradecraft: Canada at GATT, 1947–1967. *Canadian International Journal, 52*(4), 581–608.

Hart, M. (2002). *A trading nation: Canadian trade policy from colonialism to globalization*. Vancouver: UBC Press.

Hausmann, R., & Rodrick, D. (2002). *Economic development as self-discovery*. Cambridge, MA: Harvard University, Kennedy School of Government.

Heiskanen, V. (2004). The regulatory philosophy of international trade law. *Journal of World Trade, 38*(1), 1–38.

Helfer, L. (2004). Regime shifting: The TRIPs Agreement and new dynamics of international intellectual property lawmaking. *Yale Journal of International Law, 29*(1), 1–83.

Helleiner, E. (2006). *Towards North American monetary union? The politics and history of Canada's exchange rate regime*. Montreal: McGill-Queen's University Press.

Heritage Canada. (2003, July 8). *Government of Canada modifies its support programs for Canadian magazines and periodicals* [News release]. Ottawa: Office of the Minister of Heritage Canada.

Heritage Canada. Cultural Sector Investment Review. (2003). *Canadian content in magazines: A policy on investment in the periodical publishing sector*. Ottawa: Author.

Herman, L.L. (2005, November 3). Here's the path to a deal on softwood [Comment]. *The Globe and Mail*, p. A23.

Hilf, M., & Petersmann, E.-U., (Eds.). (1993). *National constitutions and international economic law*. Deventer and Boston: Kluwer Law and Taxation Publishers.

Hoekman, B.M., & Mavroidis, P.C. (2007). *The World Trade Organization: Law, economics, and politics*. London and New York: Routledge.

Hoekman, B., & Trachtman, J. (2007, August). *Canada-Wheat: Discrimination, non-commercial considerations, and state trading enterprises* (Policy Research Working Paper No. WPS4337). Washington, DC: The World Bank, Development Research Group, Trade Team.

Howse, R. (1998). *Settling trade remedy disputes: When the WTO is better than the NAFTA*. Toronto: C.D. Howe Institute.

Howse, R. (2002). From politics to technocracy and back again: The fate of the multilateral trading regime. *American Journal of International Law, 96*(1), 94–117.

Hudec, R. (1999a). *Essays on the nature of international trade law*. London: Cameron May.

Hudec, R. (1999b). The new WTO dispute settlement procedure: An overview of the first three years. *Minnesota Journal of Global Trade, 8*(1), 1–50.

Iapadre, L., & Formentini, S. (2005). *Cultural policies and international economic integration: The case of the European Union*. Aquila: Universita dell'Aquila.

Innis, H. (1995). The importance of staple products in Canadian development. In D. Drache (Ed.), *Staples, markets, and cultural change: Selected essays* (pp. 3–23). Montreal: McGill-Queen's University Press.

International Centre for Trade and Sustainable Development. (2005, December 7). Members strike deal on TRIPs and public health; Civil society unimpressed. *Bridges Weekly Trade News Digest 9*(42). Retrieved October 29, 2009, from http://ictsd.net/i/news/bridgesweekly/7522/.

International Centre of Trade and Sustainable Development. (2007). Canadian WTO notification clears path for Rwanda to import generic HIV/AIDS Drugs. *Bridges Weekly Trade News Digest 11*(34). Retrieved October 29, 2009, from http://ictsd.net/i/news/bridgesweekly/6568/.

Inwood, G. (2005). *Continentalizing Canada: The politics and legacy of the Macdonald Commission*. Toronto: University of Toronto Press.

Irwin, D.A. (1996). *Against the tide: An intellectual history of free trade*. Princeton, NJ: Princeton University Press.

Izundu, U. (2005, January 11). *Financial Times* briefing: The battle over aircraft subsidies. *Financial Times* [US edition].

Johnson, J.R. (1998). *International trade law*. Toronto: Irwin Law.

Keohane, R.O. (1984). *After hegemony : Cooperation and discord in the world political economy*. Princeton, NJ: Princeton University Press.

Keohane, R.O., & Milner, H.V. (1996). Internationalization and domestic politics: An introduction. In R.O. Keohane & H.V. Milner (Eds.), *Internationalization and domestic politics* (pp. 3–24). Cambridge: Cambridge University Press.

Keohane, R.O., Moravcsik, A., & Slaughter, A.-M. (2000). Legalized dispute resolution: Interstate and transnational. *International Organization, 54*(3), 457–488.

Kolhatkar, S. (2006, September). Inside the billionaire service industry. *Atlantic Monthly, 298*(2), 97–101.

Koskenniemmi, M. (2006). *Fragmentation of international law: Difficulties arising from the diversification and expansion of international law.* Geneva: United Nations International Law Commission.

Kremer, M. (2002). Pharmaceuticals and the developing world. *The Journal of Economic Perspectives, 16*(4), 67–90.

Krikorian, J.D. (2005). Planes, trains, and automobiles: The impact of the WTO "court" on Canada in its first ten years. *Journal of International Economic Law, 8*(4), 921–975.

Krugman, P. (1994). Competitiveness—A dangerous obsession. *Foreign Affairs, 73*(2), 28–44.

Lammert, C. *Modern welfare states under pressure: Determinants of tax policy in a globalizing world.* IRPP Working Paper No. 2004-01. Montreal: Institute for Research on Public Policy. Retrieved June 6, 2006 from http://www.irpp.org/miscpubs/archive/wp/wp2004-01.pdf.

Lawrence, R.Z. (2003). *Crimes and punishments? Retaliation under the WTO.* Washington, DC: Institute for International Economics.

Lee, M. (2002, October). *The future of industrial policy in a globalizing world: What are the options?* Briefing Paper Series: Trade and Investment No. 3.3. Ottawa: Canadian Centre for Policy Alternatives.

Lehner, S., Meiklejohn, R., & Reichenbach, H. (1991). *Fair competition in the internal market: Community state aid policy.* European Economy Series No. 48. Luxembourg: Office for Official Publications of the European Communities.

Lessig, L. (2004). *Free culture: How big media uses technology and the law to lock down culture and control creativity.* New York: Penguin Press.

Lindsey, B., & Ikenson, D. (2001). *Coming home to roost: Proliferating antidumping laws and the growing threat to U.S. exporters* (Trade Policy Analysis No. 14). Washington, DC: Cato Institute for Trade Policy Studies.

Lorimer, R. (1996). Book publishing. In M. Dorland (Ed.), *The cultural industries in Canada: Problems, policies and prospects* (pp. 3–34). Toronto, ON: James Lorimer & Company.

Magder, T. Film and video production. In M. Dorland (Ed.), *The cultural industries in Canada: Problems, policies and prospects* (pp. 145–176). Toronto, ON: James Lorimer & Company.

Magnus, J.R. (2004). World Trade Organization subsidy discipline: Is this the "retrenchment round"? *Journal of World Trade, 38*(6), 985–1047.

Malpani, R., & Kamal-Yanni, M. (2006). *Patents vs. patients: Five years after the Doha Declaration* (Oxfam Briefing Paper No. 95). Oxford: Oxfam International.

Mankiw, N.G., & Swagel, P. L. (2005). Antidumping: The third rail of trade policy. *Foreign Affairs, 84*(4), 107–119.

Marsden, K. (2005). *Reforming WTO subsidy rules: A better deal for taxpayers.* London, UK: TaxPayers' Alliance.

Marshall, K. (2005). How Canada compares in the G8. *Perspectives on Labour and Income, 6*(6), 18–25.

McBride, Stephen (2001). *Paradigm Shift: Globalization and the Canadian State.* Halifax, NS. Fernwood Publishing.

McGinnis, J.O., & Movsesian, M. L. (2000). The World Trade constitution. *Harvard Law Review, 114*(2), 511–605.

McInnes, C., & Lee, K. (2006). Health, security, and foreign policy. Review of International Studies, 32, 5–23.

Mearsheimer, J.J. (1994). The false promise of international institutions. *International Security, 19*(3), 5–49.

Mercurio, B.C. (2004). TRIPs, patents, and access to life saving drugs in the developing world. *Marquette Intellectual Property Law Review, 8*(2), 211–250.

Migara, K., & De Silva, O. (1994). *The political economy of windfalls: The "Dutch Disease"—Theory and evidence.* St. Louis, MO: John M. Olin School of Business.

Milanovic, B. (2005). *Worlds apart: Measuring international and global inequality.* Princeton: Princeton University Press.

Milner, H.V. (1997). *Interests, institutions, and information: Domestic politics and international relations.* Princeton, NJ: Princeton University Press.

Mundell, R.A. (1971). *Monetary theory: Inflation, interest, and growth in the world economy.* Pacific Palisades, CA: Goodyear Publishing Company.

Murphy, S.D. (Ed.). (2003). Modification of WTO rules on protection of pharmaceuticals. *American Journal of International Law, 97*(4), 981–982.

Napier, D.H. (2005). *2004 year-end review and 2005 forecast—An analysis.* Arlington, VA: Aerospace Industries Association.

North, D.C. (2005). *Understanding the process of economic change.* Princeton, NJ: Princeton University Press.

Nye, J.S. (2004). *Soft power: The means to success in world politics.* New York: Public Affairs.

Odessey, B. (2005, October 27). House panel approves repeal of Byrd Amendment after WTO ruling. *The United States Mission to the European Union.* Retrieved May 10, 2006, from http://useu.usmission.gov/Article.asp?ID=AD9985A7-77FB-4F24-8325-2AFDDABD3AD2.

OECD. 2008. *Producer and consumer support estimates, OECD database, 1986–2008*. Retrieved October 21, 2009, from http://www.oecd.org/document/59/0,3343,en_2649_33797_39551355_1_1_1_1,00.html.

Ostry, S. (2006, January 27). *Who rules the future? The crisis of governance and prospects for global civil society*. Paper presented at the conference *New geographies of dissent: Global counter-publics and spheres of power*, Robarts Centre for Canadian Studies, York University, Toronto, ON.

Park, R.S. (2002). The international drug industry: What the future holds for South Africa's HIV/AIDS patients. *Minnesota Journal of Global Trade, 11*(1), 125154.

Patented Medicine Prices Review Board (PMPRB). (2004). *Annual report*. Ottawa: Author. Retrieved August 4, 2006, from http://www.pmprb-cepmb.gc.ca.

Pauwelyn, J. (2001). The role of public international law in the WTO: How far can we go? *American Journal of International Law, 95*(3), 535–578.

Pecoul, B. (1999). Access to essential medicines in poor countries: A lost battle? *Journal of the American Medical Association, 281*(4), 361–367.

Petersmann, E.-U. (1998). GATT law and state trading enterprises: Critical evaluation of Article XVII and proposals for reform. In T. Cottier & P. C. Mavroidis (Eds.), *State trading in the twenty-first century*. Ann Arbor: University of Michigan Press.

Pharmaceutical Shareowners Group. (2004, September). *The public health crisis in emerging markets: An institutional investor perspective on the implications for the pharmaceutical industry*. London: Author. Retrieved November 1, 2009, from http://www.atmindex.org/resources.

Picciotto, S. (2003). Private rights vs. public standards in the WTO. *Review of International Political Economy, 10*(3), 377–405.

Pick, D.H., & Carter, C.A. (1994). Pricing to market with transactions denominated in a common currency. *American Journal of Agricultural Economics, 76*, 55–60.

Polanyi, K. (2001). *The great transformation: The political and economic origins of our time*. Boston: Beacon Press.

PricewaterhouseCoopers. (2004). *Global media and entertainment outlook: 2004–2008*. New York: Author. Retrieved July 14, 2004, from www.pwc.com/outlook.

Putnam, R.D. (1988). Diplomacy and domestic politics: The logic of two-level games. *International Organization, 42*(3), 427–460.

Raboy, M. (1996). Public television. In M. Dorland (Ed.), *The cultural industries in Canada: problems, policies, and prospects* (pp. 178–202). Toronto, ON: James Lorimer & Company.

Rahman, S.M.O., & Devadoss, S. (2002). Economics of the US-Canada softwood lumber dispute: A historical perspective. *Estey Centre Journal of International Law and Trade Policy, 3*(1), 29–45.

Rodriguez, F., & Rodrik, D. (2001). Trade policy and economic growth: A skeptic's guide to the cross-national evidence. In B. Bernanke & K. S. Rogoff (Eds.), *NBER Macroeconomics Annual 2000* (261–338). Cambridge, MA: MIT Press.

Rodrik, D. (2000, October). *Comments on "Trade, growth, and poverty" by D. Dollar and A. Kraay*. Unpublished manuscript, Harvard University. Retrieved October 26, 2009, from http://ksghome.harvard.edu/~drodrik/ Rodrik%20on%20Dollar-Kraay.PDF.

Rodrik, D. (2001, March–April). Trading in illusions. *Foreign Policy, 123*, 55–62.

Rodrik, D. (Ed.). (2003). *In search of prosperity: Analytic narratives on economic growth*. Princeton: Princeton University Press.

Roy, F. Canada's place in world trade, 1990–2005. *Canadian Economic Observer, 19*(3), 3.1, 3.8.

Ruggie, J.G. (1982). International regimes, transactions, and change: Embedded liberalism in the postwar economic order. *International Organization, 36*(2), 379–415.

Ruggie, J.G. (1994). Trade, protectionism and the future of welfare capitalism. *Journal of International Affairs, 48*(1), 1–11.

Samuelson, P.A. (2004). Where Ricardo and Mill rebut and confirm arguments of mainstream economists supporting globalization. *Journal of Economic Perspectives, 18*(3), 135–146.

Schneiderman, D. (2000). Investment rules and the new constitutionalism. *Law & Social Inquiry, 25*(3):, 757–787.

Schonfield, A. (1965). *Modern capitalism: The changing balance between public and private power*. Oxford: Oxford University Press.

Schwanen, D. (2001). *A room of our own: Cultural policies and trade agreements*. Ottawa: Institute for Research on Public Policy.

Skinner, B.J. (2005). *Seniors and drug prices in Canada and the United States*. Vancouver: The Fraser Institute.

Skogstad, G. (2008). *Internationalization and Canadian agriculture: Policy and governing paradigms*. Toronto: University of Toronto Press.

Slaughter, M.J. (2003). *Tariff elimination for industrial goods: Why the gains far outweigh any losses* [Background paper]. Washington, DC: National Foreign Trade Council. Retrieved May 18, 2006, from http://www.wto.org/english/forums_e/ngo_e/posp44_nftc_tarif_paper_e.pdf.

Smith, A. (1776). *An inquiry into the nature and causes of the wealth of nations* (3 vols.). Dublin: printed for Messrs. Whitestone, Chamberlaine, W. Watson, Potts, S. Watson [and 15 others in Dublin].

Srinivas, K.R. (2006, November). *TRIPs, access to medicines and developing nations: Towards an open source solution*. Working Paper No. 248. Bangalore: Indian Institute of Management. Retrieved November 1, 2009, from http://www.policyinnovations.org/ideas/policy_library/data/01492.

Stanford, J. (2007, January 2). Hewer of wood, pumper of oil. *Toronto Star*, p. A13.

Stanley, D. (2005). The three faces of culture: Why culture is a strategic good requiring policy attention. In C. Andrew, M. Gattinger, M.S. Jeannotte, & W. Straw (Eds.), *Accounting for culture: Thinking through cultural citizenship* (pp. 21–54). Ottawa: University of Ottawa Press.

Statistics Canada. (2005). *Government expenditures on culture*. Ottawa, ON: Author.

Stiglitz, J.E., & Charlton, A. (2004). *The development round of trade negotiations in the aftermath of Cancun: A report for the Commonwealth Secretariat*. New York: Columbia University Initiative for Policy Dialogue.

Strange, S. (2003). *States and markets* (2nd ed.). London: Continuum.

Sullivan, H.D. (2003). Regional jet trade wars: Politics and compliance in WTO dispute resolution. *Minnesota Journal of Global Trade, 12*(1), 71–108.

Sun, H. (2003). Reshaping the TRIPs Agreement concerning public health: Two critical issues. *Journal of World Trade, 37*(1), 163–197.

Sydor, A. (2003) *NAFTA @ 10: A preliminary report*. Ottawa, ON: Trade and Economic Analysis Division, Department of Foreign Affairs and International Trade.

Throsby, D. (2001). *Economics and culture*. Cambridge: Cambridge University Press.

Trebilcock, M.J., & Howse, R. (1999). *The regulation of international trade* (2nd ed.). London: Routledge.

Trebilcock, M.J., & Howse, R. (2005). *The regulation of international trade* (3rd ed.). London: Routledge.

Turner, M. (2003, July 31). Rich world's subsidies hitting African growth. *Financial Times*, p. 9.

Tyson, L.D. (1992). *Who's bashing whom? Trade conflict in high-technology indus-tries*. Washington, DC: Institute for International Economics.

UNAIDS (Joint United Nations Programme on HIV/AIDS) (2006). Global sum-mary of the HIV and AIDS epidemic, 2005 [PowerPoint slides]. In *2006 report on the global AIDS epidemic*. Geneva: Author. Retrieved October 28, 2009, from http://www.unaids.org/en/KnowledgeCentre/HIVData/GlobalReport/2006/press-kit.asp.

United Nations Economic Commission for Europe, Food and Agriculture Organiza-tion. (2005). *Forest products annual market review 2004–2005*. Geneva: Author.

United Nations Educational, Scientific, and Cultural Organization (UNESCO). (2000). *World culture report 2000: Cultural diversity, conflict, and pluralism*. Paris: Author.

United States Government Accountability Office. (1999). *Canada, Australia and New Zealand: Potential ability of state trading enterprises to distort trade* (GAO/NSIAD-96-94). Washington, DC: Author.

United States Government Accountability Office. (2005). *Issues and effects of implementing the Continued Dumping and Subsidy Offset Act*. Washington, DC: USGAO.

van den Broek, N. (2003). Power paradoxes in enforcement and implementation of World Trade Organization dispute settlement reports: Interdisciplinary approaches and new proposals. *Journal of World Trade, 37*(1), 127–162.

Veeman, M., Fulton, M., & Larue, B. (1999). *International trade in agricultural and food products: The role of state trading enterprises.* Ottawa: Agriculture Canada.

Verdun, A. (2008). Policy-making and integration in the European Union: Do economic interest groups matter? *British Journal of Politics and International Relations, 10*(1), 129–137.

Wade, R. (1989). What can economics learn from the East Asian success? *Annals of the American Academy of Political and Social Science 505*(1), 68–79.

Wade, R. (2001). Showdown at the World Bank. *New Left Review, 7,* 124–137.

Warner, M. (2002). Publics and counterpublics. *Public Culture 14*(1), 49–90.

Watkins, M.H. (1963). A staple theory of economic growth. *Canadian Journal of Economics and Political Science, 29*(2), 141–158.

Weiler, J.H.H. (2000). *The rule of lawyers and the ethos of diplomats: Reflections on the internal and external legitimacy of WTO dispute settlement.* Working paper prepared for the Jean Monnet Seminar and Workshop on the European Union, NAFTA, and the WTO: Advanced Issues in Law and Policy, Harvard Law School, Cambridge, MA. Retrieved November 1, 2009, from http://centers.law.nyu.edu/jeanmonnet/.

Weisbrot, M., Barker, D., & Rosnick, D. (2001). *The scorecard on globalization 1980–2000: Twenty years of diminished progress* (CEPR briefing paper). Washington, DC: Center for Economic and Policy Research. Retrieved January 27, 2004, from http://www.cepr.net.

Wendt, A. (1992). Anarchy is what states make of it: The social construction of power politics. *International Organization 46*(2), 391–425.

White, M. (2005, November 30). Drug patents are good for our health. *Financial Times* [Asia edition], p. 15.

Wild, J. (2006, January). A prolific year in patenting—2006 patent focus report. *KnowledgeLink Newsletter.* Retrieved October 29, 2009, from Thomson Reuters website: http://science.thomsonreuters.com/news/2006-01/8304714/.

Wilson, P.A. (2005). *Combating AIDS in the developing world.* New York: Earthscan for the UN Millennium Project, Taskforce on HIV/AIDS, Malaria, TB, and Access to Essential Medicines, Working Group on HIV/AIDS. Retrieved October 29, 2009, from http://www.unmillenniumproject.org/reports/tf_hivaids.htm.

Wolfe, R., & Mendelsohn, M. (2005). Values and interests in attitudes toward trade and globalization: The continuing compromise of embedded liberalism. *Canadian Journal of Political Science, 38*(1), 45–68.

World Trade Organization. (n.d.). *Understanding the WTO: Settling disputes — a unique contribution.* Retrieved October 29, 2009 from, http://www.wto.org/english/thewto_e/whatis_e/tif_e/disp1_e.

World Trade Organization. (1996). *Japan — Measures Concerning Sound Recordings* (File No. WT/DS28, WT/DS42). Geneva: Author.

World Trade Organization. (1999, April 14). *Brazil — Export Financing Programme for Aircraft: Report of the panel* (File No. WT/DS46/R). Geneva: Author.

World Trade Organization. (1999a, April 14). *Canada–Measures Affecting the Export of Civilian Aircraft: Report of the panel* (File No. WT/DS70/R). Geneva: Author.

World Trade Organization. (1999–2001). *United States — Section 110(5) of US Copyright Act* (File No. WT/DS160). Geneva: Author.

World Trade Organization. (2000, March 17). *Canada — Patent protection of phar- maceutical products: Report of the panel* (File No. WT/DS114/R). Geneva: Author.

World Trade Organization. (2000a, October 12). *Canada — Term of patent protec- tion: Report of the panel* (File No. WT/DS170/R). Geneva: Author.

World Trade Organization. (2001, November 14). *Doha WTO Ministerial Declaration on the TRIPs Agreement and public health.* Geneva: Author. Retrieved October 28, 2009, from www.wto.org/english/thewto_e/minist_e/ min01_e/mindecl_trips_e.htm.

World Trade Organization. (2003). *Implementation of paragraph 6 of the Doha Declaration on the TRIPs Agreement and public health.* Geneva: Author.

World Trade Organization. (2003a). *TRIPs and pharmaceutical patents* [Fact sheet]. Geneva: Author. Retrieved November 1, 2009, from http://www.wto. org/english/tratop_e/trips_e/factsheet_pharm00_e.htm.

World Trade Organization. (2007, October 5). *Notification under paragraph 2(C) of the decision of 30 August 2003 on the implementation of paragraph 6 of the Doha Declaration on the TRIPs Agreement and public health* (File No. IP/N/10/CAN/1). Geneva: Author.

World Trade Organization. (2009). *Dispute settlement.* Retrieved October 26, 2009, from the World Trade Organization website: http://www.wto.org/english/ tratop_e/dispu_e/dispu_e.htm.

WorldTradeLaw.net. (2000). Panel report: Canada — Term of patent protection. *Dispute Settlement Commentary.* Wellington, FL: Author.

Wright, R. (2008). *What is America? A short history of the new world order.* Toronto: Knopf Canada.

Young, A. (2004, August). Beyond zero sum: Trade, regulation, and NAFTA's temporary entry provisions [Monograph]. *Policy Matters 5*(6). Retrieved October 29, 2009, from the Institute for Research on Public Policy website: http://www.irpp.org/.

Young, L.M. (2000). U.S.–Canadian agricultural trade conflicts: Time for a new paradigm. *Estey Centre Journal of International Law and Trade Policy, 1*(1), 22–35.

Zehr, L. (2005, November 12). Big Pharma's big headache: Beating back the generics. *The Globe and Mail*, p. B4.

Zemans, J. (2004, May 14–15). *Advancing cultural diversity globally: The role of civil society movements*. Paper presented at the *Global flows, dissent, and diversity: The new agenda* conference, Université du Québec à Montréal, Montreal, PQ. Retrieved October 29, 2009, from the Robarts Centre for Canadian Studies at York University: http://www.yorku.ca/robarts/projects/global/.

Zysman, J. (1994). How institutions create historically rooted trajectories of growth. *Industrial and Corporate Change 3*(1), 243–283.

Index